Remaining Single
Well Worth The Wait

A Three-Faceted Journey
Towards Lasting Love

Valerie Shinbaum

Remaining Single: Well Worth The Wait
A Three-Faceted Journey Towards Lasting Love
by Valerie Shinbaum

Copyright © 2016 Valerie Shinbaum

Published by
Valerie Shinbaum

All rights reserved.

No part of this book may be reproduced in any form or by any electronic or mechanical means, including information storage and retrieval systems, without written permission from the author, except in the case of a reviewer, who may quote brief passages embodied in critical articles or in a review.

ISBN: 978-0-9970697-0-9
Library of Congress Cataloging in Publication Data on file

First Edition

Printed in the United States of America

Contents

Part One – Go West, Older Woman 7

    1. Getting From There To Here. 9

    2. Single In Spite Of Myself. 15

    3. Hope Springs Eternal In My Cinderella Heart. . 18

    4. Finding The Place Called Home. 21

    5. Distracted, Disappointed, And Derailed By Changes And Choices 25

    6. Healing The Wounds Of An Emotional Hostage. 32

Part Two – Back In The Game 39

    7. Dating Websites – Combining The Old And New. 41

    8. Required For Dating? Resilience! 47

    9. Tips For Men: Effort Brings Rewards 51

    10. Getting Out Of The "Friend Zone" With Men 55

    11. Real Men Do Exist. 59

    12. Alone vs. Lonely – The Mystery Of Connection 63

Part Three – A Shift In The Heart 67

    13. Pushing Back From The Table 69

14. Question For Men (Or Women,
    For That Matter): Why Lie? 73

15. Reframing Rejection 77

16. WAIT (Walk Along In Trust) And HOPE
    (Heart Open Prayers/Patience Extended) 81

17. Dating Without Desperation 85

Part Four – Here He Is: The Perfect One For Me.... 89

18. Eight Words For Love 91

19. The Websites Really Work! 94

20. I Got What I Prayed For 97

21. Letting Go Of Life Alone................. 101

22. A Change In Emotional Real Estate 104

23. My Turn For A Wedding................... 111

24. First-Time Bride At Last 115

Acknowledgments.......................... 119

About The Author 121

Foreword

Many times in my life I've made goals lists, not with any deadlines or time tables, just things I hoped would happen or that I would accomplish before I died. I don't like to call it a "bucket list" because I had this goals list idea in my mind decades before the movie with that same name was ever released.

Until recently, there were only two things on the list I had yet to accomplish: 1) publish a book and 2) get married. Obviously, one of these two goals was entirely up to me, and sure enough since you are reading this foreword, you know I made it happen.

The other goal was much more elusive and not entirely within my control. When I started the blog a few years ago from which this book has grown, on one level I was convinced I would remain single for the rest of my life. Yet on another level, I had hope of finding the right man to be my lifetime romantic partner. As much as I longed for this man, I was working toward acceptance of my life as an always on my own type of person.

I am the most surprised of anyone to now report that true love has come into my life and I am married, a first-time bride at 55 years old. Seems like there should be a clash of cymbals or some sort of fanfare for that experience. Perhaps there was, even if it was just inside my head.

Our wedding was a lovely magical day. And the next day, our lives continued onward. The ultimate truth is it's not about the months of planning for and the few hours when the "special day" actually occurs. It's the days and weeks and months and years to follow that make up the married experience.

I'm not different from who I was before. I didn't wake up the morning after the wedding transformed into a new person. The right one came along, and a new life chapter has begun. And then I had the proper ending for the blog and then it was able to become a book. First I got married, then I gave birth to this "baby" – my book.

What happens with the goals list now and going forward, you ask? Of course there are new goals. Perhaps there will be more books in my writing future – I hope so. Perhaps there will be other opportunities as yet to be presented. Just for today, I'm thrilled to share my journey with you and wish you well on yours.

Blessings to you all.

PART ONE

Go West, Older Woman

CHAPTER ONE

Getting From There To Here

I love the quote, "It's not the journey, it's the destination." I also love the quote, "A journey of a thousand miles begins with a single step." Both of these quotes get me thinking about how my life has unfolded. While I hope my life is far from over, I'm grateful for the wisdom I've acquired along the way.

I think of the self-help books I've read and personal work I've done and conversations I've had around being able to find and keep the right, lasting, loving romantic partner. That work has taken a lifetime for sure, and of course it continues. But now I realize the road I'm walking toward meeting, connecting with and holding onto that right romantic partner has become a journey of healing myself and finding my own authentic voice. Without that knowledge, I have no chance of recognizing that right person.

There is a strong streak of maverick in my personality. I never liked having bosses, sharing a room with anyone, or having to answer to others. I don't mind following rules if they make sense and the person enforcing them is someone I respect. But I know I have a very "my way works best" mentality, and in many instances this realization helped me make the next move. Whether it was finding a way to work for myself, or letting go a romantic relationship that wasn't right for me, or putting distance between myself and a friendship turned toxic, the voice inside my head that guides and assists me is part of the "my way works best" thinking.

In certain situations, this independent quality is an asset that served me in positive ways. It's how I visited all of the places I've traveled. Nobody to go with? I'll go alone. It's helped me have a home of my own. Nobody coming through the door to marry me? I'll buy my own condo or townhome. Nobody willing to give me a promotion? I'll find a way to work for myself and be successful.

For me, that voice inside my head is about my relationship with a Higher Power of my understanding. This doesn't have to be "God" necessarily. It could be known as "the Divine" or "the Universe" or "the Source," whatever term works for you. But in my writing and thinking I refer to that presence in my life as a Higher Power (or HP) that is my personal connection with something larger than myself, and I have an awareness that the help and guidance and support I get from HP has been a very big part of my life journey ever since my childhood.

Back to the maverick thing in my personality. When it came to romance and dating, I often heard over the years "you intimidate men." That used to hurt my feelings until I realized it's not at all accurate. Here's the real deal – if a man is intimidated by me, that's not my issue. It's his issue. I always believed the right man for me to partner with romantically would be able to see from the first moment that I am actually not an intimidating person. Do I have a strong personality? Yes. Do I have a direction, a purpose, am I a force to be reckoned with? No question. But I don't go around deliberately intimidating others. I actually have a soft side, a sensitive side, a goofy side, a tender side. Anyone who takes even a few moments to get to know me will see all of these other sides. However, anyone willing to take the time to know me has to be a strong, integrated personality type as well.

Some of this push-back in my personality has to do with my relationship with my mother, the domineering and controlling parent with whom I always had emotional conflict. In those interactions I usually felt unheard, misunderstood, and unloved. I carried these feelings into other relationships, and I know the primary original one with my mother is very much at the core of how things went wrong for me in various life situations. Specifically, I had difficulty with romantic relationships and friendships because I always thought I needed to report to her about my life. I was looking for approval and support of my choices. For her, it was an opportunity to control those same choices and leave me doubting myself because of her disapproval.

This primary relationship and its accompanying conflicts have worked my head and my heart for what seems like forever. It took a lot of individual therapy and 12-step program recovery work for me to understand myself and my needs so much better. Hurtful though this truth might be, I recognize my mother was never capable of being the kind of loving, accepting, trustworthy parent I yearned for and needed.

For decades I attempted repeatedly to try that one more thing. I would think, "Maybe if I do this nice thing she will be nice to me." It never worked. I finally had to come to a place of acceptance and find ways to build better boundaries between us. I also learned emotionally letting go of my biological mother meant my HP could bring other mother figures into my life. Today I have those much more meaningful and sustaining relationships with other mothers, who can be there for me in a way my mother could not. These special women honor my feelings, celebrate my courage, comfort my sadness and warm my heart.

On some level I must have always known there would come a time when I would choose to disconnect from the old family of origin rules for living my life, especially around my relationship with my mother. For most people this task of separation/individuation is part of normal human functioning. It's about taking what works from how I was raised and leaving the rest.

The problem for me is though I have a strong and independent personality, there is a part of me that always wanted approval, especially from my mother who I allowed to be the loudest voice in my head. This created friction between us over many years. It also created that same friction for me in other relationships with colleagues, friends, bosses, and romantic partners. For example, there were a number of things my mother didn't like about my first serious boyfriend, and I took that out on him in negative ways. I had valid reasons for breaking up with him, but my mother's opinion of him was a factor in that decision.

With my own personal work, I continue to inch my way toward healing and becoming a better person not only for myself but also for the people with whom I interact. This might not sound like a big deal, but believe me when I tell you it is. It began with my first visit to a therapist in my middle 20s who went right to mother issues. I worked with her for a short time because at that age I wasn't ready to believe my mother was not capable of giving me the kind of love that I need. Thirty years later, I finally believe this truth and have acceptance about it. It feels good and sad at the same time to have arrived at this place in my emotional travels.

It's good because I am able to move forward with more ease and success in all aspects of my life. I have a career where I am blessed to help others in this same work. I have friendships that are strong and supportive. At age 50, I moved to what I now recognize is my true home, and with that move has come a happiness I always knew was possible.

The sadness is around the need for letting go of this toxic parent. I have come to understand when there is no communication between us, I am much more at peace. In my efforts to get her to meet my love needs, there were many times when I tolerated her verbal raging or emotional manipulation.

In my times of weakness, I believed it was somehow my fault when she raged and manipulated. Today I know that's not true. It would be nice to have a birth mother who is willing and capable of loving me as a child needs. For me, that birth mother does not exist.

Thankfully, the other mothers I've been sent are women my mother's age, who are capable and willing to demonstrate the kind of love I need and deserve. Today I am open to that love from those other mothers and prefer to give my energy and attention to these women. They are there because they choose to be and I am grateful every day for their warm and positive presence in my life.

The happiness is discovering that my HP-driven choices are the best ones. Getting out from under an old toxic influence made space for new relationships with loving, gentle and accepting people who care about me. Letting go of a place where I never felt connection meant I could move to the West to my true physical, emotional and spiritual home.

For today, there is gratitude for life's journey as it continues, an appreciation of where I've come from and where I am now. One day at a time, I attempt to stay present. The reality of being single for this much of my life resonates in a profound way. I'm doing this myself, figuring out what my needs are and how to get them met. The maverick that represents the place of strength and the best part of myself believes in all things being possible.

Chapter Two

Single In Spite Of Myself

I am single, as in single, never married. For me, it's not "still single" or "sad because I'm single" or "wish I weren't single." I'm single – that's what I check in the box under marital status when I have to fill out a form at a doctor's visit or elsewhere. Sometimes I hear people say "happily single." I don't know if that is what I think – assigning a feeling to a marital status. I think I prefer to keep it simple. I'm single, never married. Yet.

Unfortunately, my marital status is burdened with some of the following definitions or nicknames – old maid, spinster, desperate, dried up, unworthy, undesirable. Quite a list of negative descriptors, don't you think? Yeah, me too. Fortunately and finally I don't see myself in any of those terms. Believe me, this was not an overnight evolvement, but rather it is an ongoing process. In this case, the journey and the destination are one and the same.

From as early on as I can remember, I always wanted a boyfriend. I always thought I would be married someday. It's those fairy stories the whole world tells mostly (if not only) to little girls. The handsome prince comes along on a white horse, rescues the girl, proposes marriage, and off they ride together. Cue the music, fade to black, happy ending, all tied up with a pretty bow.

That's what I thought I was supposed to want. Always. Sometimes I still do want that, other days not so much. But there were many times in prior chapters of my life when I felt desperate about being married, and was unbelievably sad about continuing the single journey in the world. I always wondered how it was happening over and over – the girl who always wanted the handsome prince was continually ending up on her own.

The word "alone" does not mean the same as the word "lonely," yet so often I'll hear people use the one to mean the other. Alone is a state of being, lonely is a powerful feeling. Speaking for myself, I can report being contented and comfortable at times of being alone, and I have felt achingly, desperately, heart-wrenchingly lonely at times of being surrounded by other people.

Have you ever been in a situation – a party, dance, group outing of some kind – and felt that feeling? You know the one, the one where people are all around, but you have that sense that nobody is really seeing you, as if you're invisible? It's a pretty hard sensation to deal with, but that's what it's like to feel lonely in a crowd. It's also a powerful feeling to feel lonely within a romantic relationship. It can be a painful awakening – the person to whom one is devoted, committed, perhaps even married – may not be someone with whom one feels valued, connected, appreciated, loved.

Sometimes with this realization, there is an opportunity to galvanize the painful feelings into action. There are choices to consider. The person might choose counseling, either on his/her own or with the romantic partner, to explore the lonely feelings and find some resolution. The person might choose to end the romantic relationship, which can be devastating but might be liberating as well. I read an article years ago about a group for divorced women. One of the quotes in the article that resonated with me talked about how when you're single and lonely, each tomorrow might bring a different day. But if you're married and you're lonely or unhappy, each tomorrow is the same day. That's a desolate landscape for sure.

There are other times when I'm by myself, and it seems as if I'm completely alone on the planet. Sometimes I'm hiking in the woods or skiing down a slope. Sometimes I'm driving in my car early in the morning, or sitting in my house in total quiet (no tv, no music, just the usual noises a house makes like creaking floors, or the sound of the heater clicking on). And in those moments of alone, I'm not necessarily feeling at all lonely. I am content, satisfied, comfortable in my own skin. Those are happy moments, and moments when I'm grateful for my own solitude.

So single in spite of myself is about realizing my life continues to move forward, and it's a positive, fulfilling, empowered, worthwhile, very contented life. Do I have my sad days? Absolutely. Do I have my difficult moments around romance? Without a doubt. From the day-to-day perspective, my life has meaning, purpose, and positive direction forward. For that I'm grateful, and will continue this journey one day at a time. More to come.

CHAPTER THREE

Hope Springs Eternal In My Cinderella Heart

So how do I get past the whole wanting-to-be-married thing? I don't. I don't think I've ever let go of the belief (nor do I want to) that someday it will happen for me.

Maybe that's just the way I'm emotionally hard-wired. In spite of my cynical side, or my critical side, or my "Who needs this?" side, I still have that age-old belief. It's been a part of me for as long as I can remember, and sometimes it's a very strong yearning/lonely feeling. Ironically this usually means that I've just been disappointed by a man in some way. And usually it's not at the end of big romantic relationships that had some significant impact on my life. It's more often when there might have been a possibility of someone new and then it turned out to be not at all what I want or need, but rather just a big waste of time and emotional head space.

But the yearning continues. I am a romantic, and always have been. And by that I don't mean the big gestures, like flowers and candles and limos and fancy vacations. Those are all nice too, but not really the point of what being romantic is all about. Holding hands with that special someone is romantic. Doing everyday things together is romantic. It all depends on the person I'm with and what meaning he has in my life.

The thing I struggle with sometimes is being patient, especially after one of those "nope, not this one either" situations fades away. I believe (here's the hope-springs-eternal part) there is at least one pretty terrific someone out there for me for that someday thing. I just get tired sometimes of being patient and I want to give up on the whole thing. Then that yearning comes back to remind me of how much I still want that ultimate romance.

So I believe the yearning lets me know my romantic heart is alive and well, and is capable of resilience. I can and have started over with new romances. I have allowed my feelings to guide my life. I have been able to keep my heart open to the possible and I continue to do just that. It's a challenge at times, but I know I learn so much from every romance, every possibility, no matter how fleeting.

Sometimes I learn more about what I don't want. For example, I learned through trial and error not to fall for someone's potential but rather see the person for who they are. I have worked hard on being a person who brings quality and quantity to the table of life. For me, someone without this same quality and quantity would not be the right fit.

I also learned not to be in romances with men who should be clients, not boyfriends. If I find myself doing all of the listening and they know nothing about me while I know everything about them, I'm just being someone's therapist for free. That one takes practice and constant vigilance.

So what do I want today? Someone with the basics – residence, vehicle, employment of some kind. An ability to reciprocate grace and generosity. A sense of the wider world. Self-awareness, and the understanding that we are always works in progress. An appreciation for who I am and for what I do. A curiosity and willingness to be open to new experiences.

The ability to share feelings and accept/embrace the importance of the emotional aspects of a romantic relationship. Willingness to be a partner in multiple dimensions. For example, if one of us cooks then the other cleans up. Or, more importantly, that we have each other's back if and when the occasion calls for it.

Today I know the intangibles of any relationship are really what matter. I can't put my finger on specifics all the time, but I know the best relationships have been the ones where words and gestures were equally important and both were authentic, genuine, reciprocated, and heartfelt. Where life experience was the greatest teacher and both of us were aware of that. Where mutual understanding and always respect for each other were the automatic order of the day. I know when that's meant to happen in my life again in a romantic relationship, it will be worth the wait. Meanwhile, hope springs eternal in my Cinderella heart. Stay tuned.

CHAPTER FOUR

Finding The Place Called Home

I grew up on the East Coast, and lived there until February 2011, when I made an empowering and life-changing move. That was when I moved to the Denver, Colorado area, and it felt like I'd finally arrived at my true home. For me, it's the special place of safety, strength and peace.

I learned to ski in Colorado in 1997, another lifelong dream fulfilled. That was when I moved to the Denver, Colorado area, and it felt like coming home, just as written in the lyrics from the song I mentioned. I learned to ski in Colorado in 1997, another lifelong dream fulfilled. Ever since then I came out West at least once a year for a ski week. Along with that, I began to spend more time in Western states for other reasons – traveling, speaking at conferences, attending continuing education workshops with some vacation time thrown in. And every time I got on the plane to head East, I was increasingly reluctant to go back. For me, being in the Western states always felt like a better fit.

During all that time on the East Coast, I never felt like I belonged, like I fit in, like I was a part of something. It's not just because I got picked on all through school growing up, or because I didn't have many friends at that time. It had nothing to do with where I lived as an adult, nor with whom I was friendly or romantically involved. It was a feeling that I couldn't quite describe and I only began to understand it after moving to Colorado.

When I made the decision to move away from the East Coast, it was very "meant-to-be" driven. In July of 2010, I was walking alone in a state park. I remember hearing a voice in my head and it said, "Go ahead, it's time." Thus, I began the journey that brought me to Colorado. Simple as that, though I know the decision was much longer in the making, lurking deep beneath the surface of my conscious mind.

Years ago, I knew I wanted a career that was portable, something I could do anywhere, and that I wanted to work for myself. Back then, I was still thinking in terms of a romantic partner, a potential husband whose job or residence might be elsewhere, and that would be my motivation for moving to another place. As it happens, there were discussions of relocation with a couple of my past boyfriends, but I realized a move driven by their aspirations would not be a move for me. It would be about them, and that didn't work for me. Those relationships didn't work out for good reasons, some of which have to do with being focused on what I need for myself. Relocating became something I was meant to do on my own.

It's the same as the decision I made in 2004 to work for myself. I was so over having bosses who micro-managed, or who were threatened by me, or who were power hungry, or who got their jobs by means other than their merit. That decision was long in the making but at the moment it occurred, it was an easy one to make, and the transition happened quickly and relatively smoothly.

With the move to Colorado, the wheels were set in motion, and there was no doubt or fear or indecision. It became the next right thing for me, and it happened swiftly and unfolded positively. That's not to say there weren't some glitches along the way, but that's expected. At the end of the day, the boxes arrived, things were unpacked, the house was set up, the office was furnished, the paperwork got completed so I could begin work.

It's the larger sense of belonging that I found by moving to Colorado that resonates with me. It's the way in which I was made to feel welcome, something I had never known before. It's the people I have met, each with a story to tell about their own journey to Colorado, since many folks here are transplants. That's one of my favorite things about Colorado, by the way. It's the way in which I found a voice and a purpose in a number of communities in which I participate, some work focused, others centered around my favorite activities – skiing, hiking, dancing. To be received with such positive energy and appreciation is something I never knew on the East Coast. Quite a refreshing change.

Years ago, I heard therapist and author Ann Smith speak at a continuing education conference. She told a story about having found a lasting romance after years of looking. The irony was the romance came into her life only after she purchased a very large home with more bedrooms than she could ever use as a single woman. But she felt right about the decision to purchase that large house and not long afterwards met a man who had children living with him. Guess she was meant to own that house after all.

I was led to move to Colorado, knowing that to go there would create a positive change in my life. It wasn't because I knew anyone in Colorado. I made the journey for myself as I was meant to do, aware of the vision of the home I wanted. By coming to Colorado, the vision became the reality, and I am finally home.

Chapter Five

Distracted, Disappointed, And Derailed By Changes And Choices

Twice in the month or so after I first moved to Colorado I received phone calls from two different women. Upon finding out I had moved, they asked me if I moved because I met someone. That's code for did I meet a man in a romantic relationship and did I move because of the man? These women knew me quite a few years, though not well. But I'm fascinated by this assumption, because it's such old-school thinking. On the other hand, both of these women chose to be at-home wives and mothers primarily, even though they had thriving careers in which they excelled.

I understand where that question is coming from. Even still, it seems myopic to me that someone would think it unfathomable for a woman to make the choice on her own to relocate to a new place, not basing that decision on a romantic relationship in any way.

How did this thinking come to be in the popular culture? Because mothers of daughters perpetuate it, or at least mine did. And I notice with folks I meet how differently they behave toward me if/when I do have a boyfriend vs. when I don't. It seems women especially continue to do that whole fairy-tale-ending thing when thinking about our bigger-picture life plan. Regardless of how evolved we become as a gender, we still revert back to the whole belief that life is not complete without a romantic partner.

Whenever one of my romantic relationships came to an end, I spent time with my women friends verbally dissecting what went wrong and why it ended. And I did the same with my mother, who was only too eager to pick apart not only what was wrong with the ex boyfriend, but also what I did that brought the romance to an end.

I thought at these times she was being emotionally supportive, but I realize she was fostering and encouraging a codependent, enmeshed relationship between us. In essence, if I had my mother to cry to, then what did I need boyfriends for? It was ultimately a ploy to keep me beside her so she could continue to control me and make sure I stayed her best and only friend.

In my childhood my mother did this with me around friendships in general. I always wanted to have friendships, but whenever I would tell my mother about these girls, she found something wrong with every one of them. Ironically, she wanted me to be friendly with the popular clique of girls my age who were all mean to me.

Sometimes I wonder if that was her wanting to have more popularity than she did as a child and living that out vicariously through me. But my mother did have friendships as a young girl. So why would she choose to find ways to make sure I was isolated? Again, I suspect it was because she is territorial and wanted me all to herself. It took a lot of personal work to recognize this unhealthy bond (really more like bondage) between us, and I continue to work hard at creating and maintaining clearly defined boundaries with this relationship.

Going back to letting romantic relationships drive the bus of life, I need all ten fingers and toes (and then some) to count the instances when I allowed my priorities to be influenced by what man I was involved with at the time. How often was I so wrapped up in what was going on in my romantic life (not always in a good way) that I completely put my own dreams, thoughts and personal goals to the side or let go of them altogether? Too often.

When I graduated from college, I was in my first serious romantic relationship. At the time I didn't want to move away from where I'd gone to college, but the only job offer worth taking was in New York City. My boyfriend was in Philadelphia. I went anyway, and took the job, which turned out disastrously. My boyfriend and I tried to make the long-distance thing work for a while, but it didn't last.

Looking back, I realized that first serious relationship was one of the two best of my life to date. How was I so easily able to walk away from him, when it became so difficult for me to do that with so many others for years following? Something to consider and wonder about. I chalked it up to the naive belief that if this guy was so great and he was my first serious one, the ones who would follow him would be even better. So NOT true!

Other memories float up of different men at different times. There was a man in my life when I was seriously thinking about graduate school. I put off applying to graduate school for several semesters while I waited to see what would happen with this man. He was trying to get into landscape architecture school in Virginia, and he had proposed, so I thought, "Why bother applying until I know what's going to happen with us?" Well, he and I crashed and burned, and I wound up going to graduate school in my chosen profession.

As I was finishing graduate school, there was another significant man in my life, who also talked about marriage with me quite frequently. He, too, was finishing graduate school and wanted to move to Canada, where I knew it would be difficult for me to find a job in my chosen endeavor. When I suggested a compromise, he insisted on couples therapy, in which I found out that if I were to marry this man it would be his way or no way, period. Well, that didn't work for me so needless to say, we ended. This man chose to move away – ironically NOT to Canada, but to Chicago, where he got a job. And I heard through the grapevine that about six months after we broke up he became engaged to someone. Guess I was just practice for him and I learned the heartbreakingly hard way that he was never serious about marrying me.

Another time I was with someone briefly who lived an hour away from me, and I was in the process of finding a larger condo to purchase. I actually considered moving to be near him, thinking once again that he was the ONE for me. Needless to say, he wasn't. End of story.

A major heartbreak comes to mind with a man who from the first day we met was all about having marriage conversations. For example, he would say things like, "When we get married, we will have such and such kind of wedding." He lived in a huge custom home chock-full of his man toys – collections of all kinds, a home theater, closets galore filled with his stuff, floor-to-ceiling built-in bookshelves. It was like living in a three–ring circus museum.

The only problem? No room for me or any of my things or identity, for all that this man constantly talked marriage to me. For two and a half years. Again, I put my life and dreams and plans on hold, waiting for this man to officially propose with the diamond he had shown me that was a family heirloom. He even had our parents meet each other. Who does that without being serious about sealing the deal? Yeah, I know – THIS guy! I still hadn't learned the lesson well enough, and was required to go through additional heartbreak, this one the most painful of all.

Clearly, there is a repeated pattern here – one where I jettison my own life over the side when a man comes prancing down the road. With each ended romance, I needed to go back and pick up the pieces of my own life that I'd thrown away in my hasty belief that marriage was supposed to be my goal.

A long time and many romantic relationships later, I have learned not to let go of the threads of my own life just because a romance comes my way. It's been my experience that my life continues forward as I remain single (as in never married), and the journey needs to be the one I chart for myself. Today I'm about the journey, not the destination and I know better than to believe marriage is some mythical pot of gold at the end of the rainbow. If marriage happens for me, fantastic. But not at the expense of my own interesting, full and exciting life.

A final note. In my most recent romance, which lasted five and one-half years, and with a lovely, kind, caring, intelligent and special man, I learned NOT to put anyone's life ahead of my own. I was in an exciting transition stage in my career. I was starting my own practice and working for myself. I had my own radio show. I was living in a nice home. The man I was involved with had an appreciation and acceptance for my work, my life, my goals, my plans, etc.

We had a very good five and one-half years together. From time to time I thought about moving closer to where he lived, and I even looked at places. Here again, I was almost going to give up an important part of my own life, which had to do with my location and residence. But this time, once I realized there was no investment in that process coming from his side, I dropped the idea, knowing I needed to maintain the boundary that makes my life work, both professionally and personally. As it happened, we wound up ending. The romance ran its course, and we parted ways. So there's another not-meant-to-be romance, but I wouldn't have missed it for the world.

The point is I take the life I'm given and live it to the fullest. The direction is forward, with some stops along the way, but now the train stays on the track, and there are many interesting adventures to fill the days. Will keep you posted.

CHAPTER SIX

Healing The Wounds Of An Emotional Hostage

Sometimes I set myself up to become an emotional hostage in my adult relationships. I've also been thinking about where this behavior pattern comes from and I know the answer to that question. It comes from a childhood spent as an emotional hostage of my mother who was (and still is) an angry, lonely, controlling, manipulative, judgmental narcissist, who said and did mean and hurtful things to me all through my childhood, and continues to do and say mean and hurtful things. Needless to say, she is a difficult person.

I have a favorite phrase that applies to dealing with difficult people: "Whenever you encounter a difficult person, think of that person as an angel with an assignment." Each day I work on two things that I think of as my assignments: strengthening the boundaries I need to protect myself from my mother's harsh words and actions, and healing the wounds that have resulted from this lifetime of being an emotional hostage, and have affected my adult relationships.

I understand my mother did the best she could with what she had. Her parents were similar in their affect. They made many attempts to control my mother's life throughout her childhood and her entire adult life as well. My mother's parents were raging screamers, and they raised my mother in a raging, screaming, emotionally unhealthy environment. That's what was familiar to her, and she wound up doing the same with her own husband and children.

As I grew up I also recognized I lived in two sides of my head. One side was the codependent people pleaser who wanted to avoid my mother's raging and withholding disapproval, and the other side was the individual who wanted to not be controlled by someone else, especially as I became old enough to make my own decisions.

In so many ways, this was similar to how my mother managed her life. The difference is I want to have better and healthier boundaries for better and healthier adult relationships, and live a happier life than the one my mother lives. My mother lives alone and chooses to keep herself isolated while continuing to send raging messages to me and emotionally punishing me with her words and actions. Some folks get their cardio by going to the gym or hiking or doing something else physically energizing. My mother seems to get her cardio by keeping the fires of her rage burning, and often the flames are fanned in my direction.

Where was my father during this, you might ask? I have been asked that many times and know the answer well. Any time he tried to help me or be supportive of me, my mother made sure he never heard the end of it, and she has a tongue sharper than any rapier when she chooses. I believe he did what he needed to do to protect himself from her rage also, and after all, he lived with her and I didn't. I can understand his not wanting to step in to protect me from her rage, because if he did that, the rage would be directed toward him. As it was, much of her rage was directed toward him anyway.

My dad died in 2002, and every once in a while my mother will admit she feels badly that she spent so much time toward the end of his life raging at him. Occasionally she will apologize for the mean things she does, but it is highly unusual and it doesn't mean she changes her behavior for the better. Apology means very little when no behavior change accompanies it.

I have gratitude for my relationship with my father, who was the easier parent to love. For him, all I ever needed to do was be his daughter and that was enough. I'm not saying he wasn't disappointed in me nor angry with me for things I did. But I never felt that harsh, judgmental withholding of love coming from him. When I became an adult, he believed in me and my ability to make my own choices. And he didn't beat me over the head verbally if and when I did make a mistake.

On occasion, I've attempted to explain to my mother that I don't accept her controlling, hurtful, manipulative behaviors. Then I need to remember I am dealing with a narcissist. Narcissists are rarely, if ever, willing to be held accountable for anything they do that might hurt others. They become defensive and find ways to make anything they do someone else's fault. No matter what I say or how I say it, my words will fall on deaf ears and there will be no impact whatsoever nor any change in her behavior toward me. Today I go back to my boundaries, and try to protect myself from this difficult and dangerous person.

How does this affect my adult relationships? Let's begin with romances. More often than not, I was in romances with men who were controlling, manipulative, distancing, emotionally neglectful narcissists, and I found myself bending over backwards in attempts to please these men, just as I would with my mother. Then came the moment when I recognized how much I was over doing in the relationship, and all of the effort was coming from me. At these moments I realized I was involved with someone who never would give me the love, kindness, acceptance, support, regard, respect, and understanding I want in any relationship.

Why was I with men like this over and over? Because on a visceral level they seemed familiar to me, much in the same way it must have made sense for my mother to raise me as she was raised. When something is familiar, we don't stop to consider whether or not familiar is equal to safe. Many times those two words are not equal at all. Fortunately, with the help of some personal work, I was able to break the pattern of dating narcissists. I know now that I am capable of maintaining a healthy romance over an extended period of time. Having had that, I know what to look for again and will not settle for anything less.

Sometimes I tend to be codependent with friendships as well. I am flattered when someone wants to be my friend, like a puppy who feels loved as long as someone shows it attention. But there are all kinds of attention and not all of it is positive. There are people who want to befriend me for what I bring to the friendship. Here again I need to be careful not to mistake kindness for weakness and vice versa. I have been in friendships with people who expected me to be their therapist for free. While I brought strength, honesty, and energy to the friendship, the other person was not capable of doing the same.

I know I can't expect 50/50 reciprocity in every relationship, but I need to look for balanced people with something more to offer beyond the initial kind word. Many times I hang my whole heart on that kind word and believe the person who uttered it to be the best person to know. Just as with romance, many folks are able to put on a best face at the beginning of a relationship in order to draw the other person in. But there is really nothing beneath that facade. When that realization happens, it's like having an emotional rug ripped out from under me. I feel totally off balance emotionally, unable to believe I was taken in again.

This fallout stems from a childhood of not knowing if or when the next kind word was coming along. And if kind words came along, they could be followed with the most vicious ones to replace them within the space of a few moments. Here's more of the hostage taking – if I never know where I stand, it's very easy to be knocked off balance. In certain relationships – romances and friendships – I find myself wondering about the other person, planning my activities and time around when that person would be available, and making myself available to accommodate the other person's schedule. That's the sign and signal that I am back to being codependent, to accommodate someone else at my own expense in order to preserve the relationship. Not the best situation for me. I need to remember my schedule is the one I should consider first, and the relationship I have with myself needs to be the first priority.

Someone said to me recently that in order to have a level playing field in any relationship, it's important to have an investment in who I allow into my life, rather than just taking whatever comes along, like that puppy who so wants to be cared for and loved. I am grateful to the person who shared that thought with me, and am taking it to heart each day, as I continue to strive toward healthier choices with any type of relationship.

Believe it or not, I have gratitude for my mother as well. I am grateful she decided to have children and chose to give birth to me, raise me and make sure I became an independent adult. I am grateful for everything positive I learned from her. I am even grateful for the negative things about her because I can use those as examples of how I don't want to be toward other people. In the past, I used to take things out on others as she frequently does. I know how much this hurts and I have worked hard to change my behavior so I no longer displace my anger. If I have a hard day, I don't come home and kick the dog, so to speak.

Another of my favorite phrases is: "Say what you mean, mean what you say, don't say it mean." Having grown up with someone mean, I work hard at honing my verbal delivery, and to try to think before I speak. I don't always do this as well as I would like, but each day is another opportunity to practice, practice, practice. That's what I do with each friendship or romance. When friendships or romances end, I know this means there will be new and perhaps better, healthier friendships or romances brought to me to replace them. Doors never close without windows opening somewhere else, and each new experience is another opportunity to avoid being taken emotionally hostage. The healing continues daily.

PART TWO

Back In The Game

CHAPTER SEVEN

Dating Websites – Combining The Old And New

Yes, I use dating websites. This is not new to me. I believe dating websites to be just as viable for finding a romantic relationship as any other venue. How many times do I hear people say they met in a bar? Where there's alcohol involved? And where perceptions might be impaired by said alcohol? And many of those relationships lead to lasting positive partnerships, even though there is quite the risk considering the possible obstacles. So what's the difference between something like that turning into true love vs. any other romantic–possibility delivery system? Hence, the dating websites.

The best and longest-lasting romantic relationship of my life was with a man I met by chance on a group trip in Europe. Just before I met him, I had been doing the dating website thing for quite a while, at least a year continuously. I was on a few sites and met a number of men, but nothing had clicked into a long-term romance.

About a month before I met my ex-boyfriend, I had hit a wall, so to speak, with the whole dating thing and had decided to stop using the dating websites. And then, a month later just about to the day from my last dating website date, along came true love – and at the moment when I was not actively looking for it any more.

Does that mean I can't find the next right romance through a dating website, or through any other mechanism that seems like I'm actively looking vs. letting fate or destiny do the deciding? I always say there is no difference between using a dating website and any other type of website to gather information before deciding whether or not to proceed further with something.

I've used websites to find office space, buy a home, choose a plumber, research vacation spots, write reviews for restaurants and hotels, and thousands of other things. It's all about information exchange and knowing what choices/options are available. Why would I not take advantage of that same information-gathering type of site to do the same kind of deciding? Seems like a no-brainer to me.

Of course there are numerous horrible dating stories told about people who met through Internet dating sites. I have a number of them myself from prior experiences with online dating. I have an equal number of horrible dating stories from experiences NOT found through Internet dating sites. Don't even get me started on fix ups, for example. Thankfully, I haven't been fixed up in a very long time.

When I fix people up, I do it based on a feeling, or an instinct, and I don't do it unless I have a really strong sense that the two people I'm fixing up will hit it off. Twice I've been right about that. Once was about 20 years ago, and that couple got engaged nine months later. More recently I had an opportunity to fix up two people, again based on that instinct or feeling, and again it went well, and they are romantically, happily together. On the other hand, when folks have fixed me up, they seem to have used what I call the "Noah's Ark" approach to fix ups. It goes something like this: I'm a woman, he's a man, we're both heterosexual and single with a pulse so therefore, we're a match! Good gracious, what were those people thinking?

For every horrible dating experience anyone can share – again, including myself – from dating websites, there are just as many good stories of romantic lasting love found through those sites. I'm not going to rule anything out, and that includes the dating sites. And this time I'm thinking I'll stick and stay instead of walking away, because I have learned it's important to have patience and persistence with most things in life.

Here's an example. I learned to ski at 37 years old. It's harder to learn a sport as a grownup, fear factor being what it is, and skiing is not easy to pick up. But from the very first time I ever went, terrified as I was, the whole experience was thrilling for me at the same time. I mostly fell down throughout the first four years of my ski career but I didn't give up. I kept coming back for more, and now years later, I'm a good skier and I still love it. I teach other people to ski, and they wind up loving it too. It's just as thrilling for me now as it was in the beginning, only now it's even better because I actually know what I'm doing and I have a blast doing it.

It's the same thing with dating, in my opinion. I can allow fate or destiny to drive the bus, or I can give it a little push, get out there and do some driving on my own, or at least ride shotgun. That's where I see the combination of the old and new. Dating websites are all about communication between two people, at first by correspondence. How is this any different from letters written by potential romantic partners in centuries gone by?

Jane Austen used letter writing as a device in many of her novels, to drive the fate of the potential lovers forward. One of my favorites is at the end of "Persuasion" when Captain Wentworth leaves a letter for Ann to find. In this letter, he declares his feelings for her and gives her instructions about what the next step would be if she should return his affections. So romantic.

Long before the Internet, I was a letter writer. I kept in touch with friendships I made at summer camps, knew in college, and with people I met on vacation or elsewhere. There were ex-boyfriends and potential romantic partners who were great letter writers. Years ago, I got a letter written by a fellow who was crushing on me, all written in rhyme. It was beautiful. We never did quite get into a romance, but I still remember how clever that letter was. I've always enjoyed sending and receiving letters. And now with email, I am able to stay in touch with different people from all over the world, and with much quicker response time. That's a treat for sure.

So there's the combination of the old and the new. We're still using written correspondence as an exercise in getting to know someone better. I appreciate the eloquence of many emails I've received. Some of them have inspired me to be eloquent as well. Sometimes I save these email exchanges as reminders for myself of the stories I tell, and of the responses those stories receive. These days it's not important who makes the first contact. It's the use of the old in that we're using the power of the written words to make contact. The new speaks not only to the technology but also to the modern thought that no longer are women forced to wait for a man to come to them. I have found many men are just as indifferent to who initiates the contact as I am. A refreshing blend of old and new.

Back to the idea of choosing once the options are better known. This dating website method allows us to conduct a correspondence before making a commitment to meet face to face. It also allows us to be in contact with folks who might not live right around the corner, but who's to say they might not be a perfect fit?

In the best of the scenario outcomes, the emails lead to phone calls, the phone calls lead to face-to-face meetings, the face-to-face meetings might lead to the next great romance. I've certainly heard enough of the positive–outcome stories to help my hopeful romantic side continue to believe in the power of the possible.

How can one not be hopeful from what seems like a foolproof method? Here's where some of the horrible stories come in. There are people who lie. I know, big surprise, right? There are people who want nothing more than the correspondence online without the phone calls or face-to face-contact. There are some folks who can do the email and the phone thing, but face to face freaks them out and they run or disappear. I have had some meet-and-greet first dates that were lovely and then I never saw or heard from them again.

I realize dating can be difficult and even scary, not because of who is out there, but because of their lack of emotional readiness and willingness to be vulnerable with someone else. And that's all right, because if someone isn't willing or open and vanishes early on, he's doing me a favor because he's getting out of the way of the better potential romantic partner I've yet to meet.

For every negative outcome story there can be just as many on the positive side of the aisle. I look at all of these adventures with a great deal of gratitude, because with each encounter I learn something about myself. I learn what I do want and what I don't want. I learn that I have just as much right to say "no thanks" as a man does. I learn I have the capacity to be open and willing, and I'm able to trust myself. And if something doesn't work out, that means something better might be in the next email I send or receive. I didn't give up on skiing and it was worth it. I don't choose to give up on dating websites. And a side benefit is I have a collection of interesting stories, which is always a plus!

CHAPTER EIGHT

Required For Dating? Resilience!

I can't think of a better word when it comes to dating. How else would someone be able to bounce back from heartbreak, rejection, disappointment and all of the other elements involved in the dating dance?

Let's start at the beginning with the dating websites. Creating a profile takes time, work and effort. It's no different from creating a resume for a job search, and in fact at times the whole dating/relationship search feels just like a job search. Just as with a job search, there are questions to answer, profile statements to write, photos to post – all in an effort to sell oneself in the best possible light.

One of the things I've learned about job searches is along with selling myself via resumes and job interviews, I also was deciding whether or not a certain employment opportunity was right for me at the same time. I need to remember I am doing as much of the deciding as men are about who might be a right romantic fit for me. I don't see that as negative but rather as empowering.

The next step is to browse through profiles of men on the sites and decide if any of them are worth contacting. At first it feels like being a kid in a candy store. What a treat to have access to so many men who sound so interesting at first glance. But after a while, the majority of the profiles start to sound or seem the same. And sometimes the language of the profile will indicate it's written by a scammer. Scammers are on all of the sites, so it's impossible to avoid them. That's one of the drawbacks of website dating. But there are just as many people who lie in real life as there are on websites, so that's not unique to website dating at all.

On to the next step – deciding whether or not to contact someone. I'm old school in that I enjoy being wooed, but I have no problem reaching out to someone to initiate contact. I appreciate men who appreciate that about me in fact. After the decision is made to put an email out there, then comes the hardest part – waiting to see if he'll answer back. Many times they don't answer at all. Many times they answer once, but never again. Sometimes they reach out and a dialogue is begun, but it never goes beyond email contact. Then there are the men who are email and phone only, but when an effort is made to get together in real life, they vanish like smoke in the wind. Resilience is necessary here for the frustration that comes from wanting more and the more never happens.

Perhaps there might be a face-to-face date planned that actually happens. Here again, resilience is required because a first date is something to look forward to, but when it actually happens, the realization that there won't be a second date brings up feelings of disappointment. Even if it's a choice to keep it at one and done, it's still a letdown after the buildup of looking forward to the possibility of the situation igniting romantic sparks.

Sometimes things do progress to more dates, and sometimes even beyond more dates to that actual romantic spark beginning. That's lovely when it happens, but here again, the need for resilience is important, because a romance might be short-lived. There are so many mixed messages out there and so many folks who say they are looking for "the one" but are really playing the field. Or there are folks who might think they want "the one" but are not emotionally ready for what that means. Then, there are folks whose lives have way too much chaos for them to even think about dating and yet they are among the ranks as well. Again, resilience is important because at any of the above stages, the weeding-out process is happening on both sides. People might take things so far, only to back off and disappear. In order not to be emotionally devastated by that if/when it happens, it's essential to operate from a place of resilience.

We can't always figure this out right at the beginning. It takes time to get to know someone, obviously. The red flags don't always start flying right away. I've learned to be more up front about the red flags when I notice them. I didn't do that in the past, much to my misfortune. Had I paid attention to the red flags in certain situations, I might have avoided some major heartbreak. On the other hand, because I operate with resilience, I have an opportunity to learn from each experience, even the ones that are so hurtful and cause me emotional pain.

An example that comes to mind is a man with whom I had daily phone contact for a month. This man and I engaged in hours-long conversations, and it was lovely and seemed heartfelt. Somehow the red flag of his never being able to meet in person didn't really hit me until I'd fallen for his excuses three different times. I so wanted to believe in this man, wanted to trust that he was really available for me. Sadly, this was not the case. By the third of our attempts to make plans to meet face to face and him bailing, I realized the whole situation was never going to go where I'd hoped it would.

I'm not saying there wasn't something good about it. I allowed my heart to be open to someone, allowed myself to feel feelings for someone that had long since been shut down or closed off. Here's where resilience comes in as the lesson learned. I survived the experience, moved on to other dating experiences and appreciated that at least for a month of my life I was being kept company by a man who, even if he was only a voice on the phone, seemed to care about me, my life and my worth. Taking away something positive from what turned out to be negative is the way in which resilience is useful.

The thing about emotional pain is it helps with the growth process. Because I have resilience, I allow myself to feel the pain and eventually step back from it. I see the experience for what it was and how it helped me. Then I have gratitude that the experience came to an end. One of my favorite sayings is, "The Universe never closes a door in one place without opening another one somewhere else." I believe this with all my heart. And with gratitude for being blessed with resilience, I get back on the horse and keep on riding forward.

CHAPTER NINE

Tips For Men: Effort Brings Rewards

Of course I'm a modern woman. What does this mean? It means I don't mind making the first move to contact a man, flirt with a man, or reach out to make a connection with a man. I'm fine with being someone who does that. In other areas of my life, I don't hesitate to make a move, whether that's buying a house or a car, making plans with friends, organizing a group event, renting office space, or planning a vacation.

Whatever comes up in the rest of my life, I do it for myself, which is empowering and strengthening. I haven't been one to wait and sit back for someone else to do for me. Being single throughout my entire adult life has taught me a lot about being self-sufficient and self-reliant.

When it comes to dating, I'm in a place where reaching out to men isn't scary and it doesn't feel wrong for me to be the one who initiates. As with anything else in life, if something seems possible with a man in terms of potential romance, I have no problem being the one to say how about coffee, or a hike, or whatever. Sometimes there is follow-up and sometimes there is not, but I am a firm believer in helping fate along instead of sitting back and waiting for it to do all the work. I'm always open to the possibilities of fate, but while I'm waiting, I can be out there dating too, right?

At the same time, I love it when a man is capable of courting in the old school way, and this is where I'm a big fan of the effort. What is the effort about, you ask? I'll give you examples from some of my recent online dating adventures. It starts with reaching out via email, and saying something more than "Hi." When I talk to younger folks who are Facebook fanatics, I hear from them that the standard opening line is "Hi." That may be true, but really, does a man think I'm going to respond to something as simplistic as that? Effort, fellows! Ask me a question, comment about something you read in my profile, send me a signal that you're interested in me, and let me know you hope I'll write you back.

Here's another one. I know the young folks are all about text, and I'm hip to that too, but I very much enjoy when a man calls and we have a voice-to-voice conversation. Here again, effort wins points with me. The opportunity to hear a voice and make that initial connection on the phone helps me decide if I want to take the next step and see if he's worth meeting in person.

Further, the men who call when they say they're going to call get points too. There's nothing better than a man who demonstrates reliability at least initially by something as simple as being true to his word. And once we're on the phone and talking, he knows the value of a reciprocal conversation, one in which we are asking each other questions to get to know each other. Reaching for that connection makes such a positive difference.

Next step – he's up for making a plan to get together instead of going back and forth with endless emails or phone calls about wanting to get together but not having any time. Men, take note – I'm just as busy as you are, and my life is just as interesting and full. So I'm not impressed with words about being too busy to call or email or make a plan. It seems like ducking, making excuses, or perhaps game playing. If you're serious about getting to meet someone, then be real with yourself and me and let's make the plan for the meet.

I find frequently there are men who may put it out there initially that they want to meet, but somehow there are numerous excuses communicated through email that their lives are so busy, etc., etc. And then they say they will be in touch to make a plan for a meeting. I don't waste a lot of my time with men like this. The men who get my attention are the ones who commit to making a face-to-face meeting happen.

When the meeting happens, I enjoy other old-school gestures. Sometimes a man brings me flowers. They may be from the grocery store, but who cares? It's still a classy thing to do, along with holding doors for me, or offering to pay if a meal is involved. Again, it goes a long way in earning points.

And what I mean by points doesn't mean some physical reward, like sex on the first date. That's not what it's about. It's about my respect, my genuine interest in getting to know you, my gratitude for taking the time to be positively attentive, just as I am doing the same with you. The dates I enjoy most are the ones where the men make the kind of effort that is memorable, and leaves me hoping they'll call me again.

And fellows, if you do, don't forget to bring that effort. I promise it's worth it.

CHAPTER TEN

Getting Out Of The "Friend Zone" With Men

I hate when I get "friend zoned" by men I'm interested in romantically, and that is so NOT what I want! I need to stay out of the friend zone, because it is a mixed message and a game I don't have any interest in playing. My intention in being out in the dating world is to find a man with whom I can form a healthy romantic partnership, and together we will grow a relationship that is lasting, monogamous, committed, and happy. No interest in being the "friend zone" girl here.

I am quite familiar with the "friend zone" situation. For decades I was the "friend girl," which means I'm the one men would talk to about girls they wanted to be involved with romantically. This drove me crazy, because it meant spending time with men I was attracted to or interested in romantically, but they wanted no part of me in that way. I am sure I don't have to tell you how frustrating it is to be relegated to the "friend zone" over and over again.

Being "friend zoned" repeatedly had an impact on my dating choices, and not always in a positive way. In several instances I entered into romantic relationships that weren't right for me, but I remember feeling relieved that someone wanted to be romantically involved with me instead of sending me to the "friend zone." I had to examine that and understand myself well enough to know it's worth the wait for the kind of a romance I want rather than just relief because some man saw me as more than just a friend.

The thing is, I already have enough friends in my life. I have some friends who are men, but they are more what I would consider to be acquaintances. They are men I know from shared activities. However, for the most part, I don't actively seek them out to do things outside of those activities.

I also have women acquaintances from shared activities. Here's the difference – I'm more likely to reach out to a woman acquaintance and grow a friendship from there than I would with a man from a shared activity. That's my preference, because there is no likelihood of someone reading something into that situation that might not be shared on both sides.

I find there are many men who are confused about what they want. Sometimes it's because they are still hurt by a past romance. Sometimes they are taking the next step beyond that hurt to look at what part they played in the demise or failure of that past romance. I have respect for that, having done work like that throughout my life.

But sometimes the messages they send are more confusing than they might realize. They might not recognize they are sending a flirty message, or a message that they might be interested romantically. It's like they are dipping their toes in the pool to see how the water feels. I know today I don't want to be someone's consolation prize. I am not someone's "pool" in which they can "test the waters."

So how to avoid the "friend zone?" There is no avoiding being told someone wants to be "just friends" but if/when they do say that to me, I choose to say no thanks. I am not mean about it, nor am I hurtful with them. I just know I don't want to pursue anything more with any man who "friend zones" me, because right away I know that man is not anywhere near ready for what I want. No point in starting a relationship with someone who isn't on the same page from the start, right?

At this stage in my life I'm so over being tense and frustrated by mixed signals with men. Any man who can't come right out and say he's interested in a romance with me is not a man with whom I want or need to have any involvement. In my best former romantic relationships, communication was direct and open from the start. I didn't have to guess or wonder what the intention was.

A friend of mine recently reminded me of something she saw on a talk show. She said an author of self-help books was saying that if a man says he's not ready to be in a romance, believe him! Good advice in my opinion. I can't help being interested in men romantically. But if they say clearly they are not ready, they are telling me they are not interested. If a man is interested in me romantically, he will make the move to let me know. That's worth waiting for, instead of wasting time in the "friend zone."

CHAPTER ELEVEN

Real Men Do Exist

I enjoy hearing love stories because they renew my hope and faith that a "real man" does exist for me out there somewhere. My parents had a good love story. They were introduced by a mutual acquaintance. They were not living in the same area, and yet they managed to connect, fall in love, get married and stay married for 45 years until my dad's death. And their courtship/romance was in 1956 and 1957, before cell phones, Skype, email, and all of the other modern technological conveniences we have today.

A dear friend of mine tells a similar story about her parents. Three weeks after they met, my friend's dad asked her mom to marry him, but she said no because they had known each other for only three weeks. But he said he was heading off to World War II and wanted her for his wife. She again said no, but did promise to wait for him. Well, she did, for the whole of World War II. When he returned from the war, he proposed in January, they were married in February and my friend was born in December of that year.

Years ago, I read the "Little House" series by Laura Ingalls Wilder. What always struck me was that Laura's parents had what I call a partnership. I always enjoyed reading these stories for the way Pa appreciated Ma, and that appreciation was reciprocated. They worked hard together on everything they did. Whether it was packing up their wagon to move the family to a new place, building a house together once they got to the new place, or Ma making a wholesome meal for the family, I always got the impression that their respect and regard for each other was genuine and lifelong.

Some might say those stories exist only from back then, but I just finished reading another love story written by a woman who is in her 40s and lives in Oklahoma on a ranch with her husband and four children. She is a food show host and blogger, and decided to write the story of the romance between herself and her husband and how they wound up together.

And this story takes place in today's world. This woman was courted by what I describe as a "real man." They met in a bar, she was instantly smitten, and they talked together for a while that first night they met. Four months later he called her and asked her for a date and it was game on, so to speak, from that moment. They fell hard for each other and the story is a powerful read, though simple at the same time. The reason it resonates so much with me? Because it harkens back to the stories of my parents or my friend's parents, or similar stories I've heard over the years.

What is the common factor? That the men involved were what I again refer to as "real men." They were men who knew themselves and exactly what they wanted for their own lives. They were men who had a direction, a purpose, a role in life they knew they were meant to play. They were men who didn't need to be unsure of themselves and didn't think finding a woman to love and cherish is such a hard prospect. They were not game players or liars. They were men who meant what they said and didn't mince words. They put their hearts out there and weren't afraid to declare their feelings for the women they chose to love. And having declared their love, they continued or continue to appreciate their women, to respect them, to admire them, to value their lives and the partnership that grew between them.

The details of the stories are not important. The common factor again is these couples experienced partnership in romance, which is worth the time it takes to find. It's what I know I'm waiting for. In order for a romantic partnership to exist, each person needs to be aware of who he/she is, of what is important and valuable in his/her own life. There are no games, no guessing, but rather trusting instinct and knowing the other person is doing the same. It's not that complicated when you think about it, is it?

So much has been written about ways for men and women to change themselves in order to find lasting love. I don't think changing oneself is really the answer. Rather I think it's more important to be honest about who we are. To be clear about what we want, and to be contented with where our lives are right at the moment, romantic partner or not. And then to be able to say what does and doesn't work for us.

I made a promise to myself a long time ago that I would not settle for anything less in my life than what I wanted, and that's with regard to career, where I live, the activities I enjoy, and the friendships I choose. I've become better at keeping that promise, with a number of positive outcomes.

I have a spiritual connection with a Higher Power who guides, protects, challenges, and sends me everything I'm meant to have. I am blessed to have that same Source remove things or people from my life when the lessons learned from those experiences are revealed. When my Higher Power removes things or people, I am convinced this makes room for even better things or people to come into my life, part of that ongoing evolution that is my own journey. My daily goal is to be an authentic, integrated, contented, joyous "real woman." I am not looking for someone else to be responsible for my happiness. I know it's up to me to create that in my own life.

With that said, I continue to believe there is a "real man" out there for me somewhere. He is as committed to his own walk through this world as I am to mine. He is looking for a "real woman" just as much as I am looking for a "real man" and when the timing works, then we will meet. Don't know where, don't know when, but that doesn't matter. I'll keep moving forward and keep my heart open. The "real man" and I will know it when we meet. And then we'll continue moving forward together.

Chapter Twelve

Alone vs. Lonely – The Mystery Of Connection

One is a state of being. There are many points in a lifetime when a person is alone. The other is a feeling, one with which we're hardwired from birth. So why is it so hard for us to acknowledge and accept the difference between "alone"and "lonely?" Because the word lonely is something people don't want to say. Even the word alone brings up painful or hurtful memories and old emotional wounds. Yet one word doesn't always lead to the other. The two are totally different concepts.

Think about all the things we do alone on a regular basis. Often we drive to various places alone – food shopping, the gym, work or school, doctor or dentist, etc. We spend much of our lives alone, even if we are emotionally or physically connected to others. Some of us choose to work alone. In any of these instances, alone doesn't come with the negative image driven by fear, anger, or sadness.

We can be lonely even when we're not physically alone. I felt lonely throughout my entire life, and like anyone else, I've been surrounded by or interacting with other people constantly. There are lonely times I can point to when I felt lonely, even when I was with others. The trigger of lonely feelings for me is when I have a sense that I am not being heard, understood, validated, accepted, or supported. Often my reaction to lonely feelings is to cry.

It used to bother me when the crying thing would happen. Now I look at it as the gift of a physical response that sends a signal, telling me to remove myself from whatever situation is generating those lonely feelings. Whether it's a work situation, family-of-origin dynamic, romance or friendship, if I'm in tears about it, then it's time to let it go.

There is a part of me that yearns to connect with others. I have no problem wearing my heart on my sleeve. I don't hold back from displaying feelings and am comfortable in my own skin. I can take accountability for my character defects and strive to be present, conscious, and willing.

Sometimes I need my alone time. I need to regroup after I've been hurt by people, whether it be in romance, work, family of origin, or friendship. I need the alone times to be reminded that I can trust in and depend on myself.

At these times I also do the spiritual work of connecting with the Source or Higher Power who helps guide me through the necessary step of sitting with the lonely feelings. It's the healing process for the emotional hurts, and the rebuilding of self-confidence and self-awareness that will hopefully lead to a better outcome the next time.

I recall a community dance where a newly married couple arrived after their wedding reception. At the end of the dance, the band played a waltz and the wedding couple was invited to come on the floor and take the first turn by themselves as the rest of us stood at the edges watching and applauding. It was such a sweet and romantic moment.

Watching these two glide through the first part of the waltz so beautifully together, I was aware of how I cherish these precious romantic moments, being such a romantic myself. Then came the powerful lonely feeling, along with sadness and yearning. Though I've been single my entire adult life as in never married, that doesn't mean I ever stopped hoping, wishing, wanting and waiting for that special romantic partner to be in my life, to share my life, to witness my life, and to whom my life would matter.

Thankfully, I have a support network of people who hear me, understand me, and validate me. Yet there is still that one relationship that enhances a life in a different way, the romantic partner who is a different kind of witness from the others mentioned here.

What is it that makes me continue to yearn for this one special person? Hard to say. Most of the time I like my life the way it is for many reasons. All of these years on my own have given me the opportunity to be comfortable and content with myself, to be at peace with the knowledge that it might just be me day in and day out.

Several times in my romantic past I was with men for whom marriage was a frequently discussed topic. Once or twice there was even a proposal in the midst of those discussions. But with every situation, there was a reason not to pull the trigger, and I know it was coming from within me. I had the instinct to keep going, to be able to be alone again (even if occasionally lonely) instead of with someone for whom I would not be a top priority.

When those yearning feelings come up for me, I recognize how much I still wonder about the possibility of the romantic someone finding his way into my life. It's not just about any man. It has to be the right romantic someone. And while I don't have a checklist because I know better than to work that way, I do have the firm belief and commitment to myself that I won't settle just to be with any someone. It's a much longer wait when it's not about settling. When it's about the special things I know I need, want, and deserve, it's going to come whenever that's meant to happen and I don't have control over that process.

All I need to remember is to live the life I have. I choose to be grateful for the feelings of sadness, loneliness and the yearning for that special romance like no other. I know my worth in the world, and the gifts I'm given during this time on Earth. When I choose to trust the process of believing in Higher Power's larger plan, I have awareness that more will be revealed. That's the moment when I'm comforted in the knowledge that the lonely feeling will pass, and I am not alone.

PART THREE

A Shift In The Heart

CHAPTER THIRTEEN

Pushing Back From The Table

At times, doing the active dating thing seems like taking on a work project, or searching for a house to buy. It comes with exhausting moments, in my experience. Does that exhaustion mean I am giving up, or getting cynical about it? Not at all, but I do go through periods of fatigue around it. Again from experience I am able to recognize that's the larger Presence/Universe telling me to push back from the table for a moment and take a breath.

That's what I chose to do after 14 months of being focused, directed, and really out there. I was sending out emails, initiating lots of contact with different men, and going on lots of first dates. Occasionally I had more than one date with the same man. Even less frequently there was a glimmer of potential romantic relationship possibility. Once or twice it seemed as if that romantic connection might have led to an actual relationship.

Overall, nothing lasted long term, but somehow more than a year of this dating website experiment had come and gone. Yet I was no closer to a long-term, monogamous, lasting, special, meaningful romantic relationship. I refer to this time in the dating journey as some nice kisses but mostly near misses. Some of this was about what message I was putting out there. As I pushed back from the table, I took the time to do an emotional reset, a closer look at whether or not I was really ready for the kind of relationship I thought I wanted.

I've read women always need to learn something from every romantic relationship experience. For me, that's true of all experiences. In this time of pushing back, I took a closer look at my recent foray into the directed dating world, and at significant past romances. Additionally, it was time to review relationships in other areas of my life. Certain people who I thought of as friends were not really friends at all. I was still connecting with or attaching to folks who should have been clients in my professional life as a psychotherapist. I went back to work on setting stronger emotional boundaries.

There was a need to push back on the emotional boundary issue with my mother as well. She came for three visits in the first year after I moved West. The first two visits went well. The third? Not so much. At the end of that visit, I remember feeling emotionally hung over, and breathing a sigh of relief that she'd gone. That third visit sparked a recognition of the need to move toward a disconnect between me and my mother. I knew Higher Power was presenting more evidence about the true nature of her character. It wasn't about blaming; it was way beyond that. Rather, I was coming to better acceptance of who my mother is – someone who has very little capability to be for anyone else other than herself.

In the second year of living in Colorado, I again invited my mother to visit, and she kept turning me down. At first, my mother's excuses for not visiting seemed valid. Then it struck me that she was deliberately choosing not to come. I felt hurt by this, but still didn't know how to give her up completely, even though I began to push back from her emotionally in my own head. I didn't share with her as often about my life, and it felt good to strengthen that boundary.

This boundary helped me with other relationships. I saw parallels between the way my mother judges me harshly or critically and how I allowed certain others to do the same. I did a lot of pushing back and cleaning house with friendships after that first 14 months of directed dating. I got better at holding my ground regarding unacceptable behavior in all situations. The best outcome from this endeavor? Every time I'm empowered to let go of failed romances or unhealthy friendships, I make space for new and hopefully better possibilities.

Back to lessons learned in the dating arena. In this most recent attempt to find lasting love, I discovered there are many men out there. For anyone who says it's hard to meet men, I respectfully disagree. In my experience, there are men everywhere, and not just on the dating websites. It's not at all difficult to find quantity. Quality, however? That's more of a challenge, requiring patience, persistence and willingness to be open. I had some profound heartbreak with a couple of romantic encounters as well as with friendships at this time. While it was so painful, I was relieved to be able to feel my feelings again, which I hadn't been able to do for years. They were more intense than at any other time in my life, and I didn't mind. At least now I knew what to shoot for.

A very dear friend of mine talks about how we all have "time people" in our lives. The concept is that a person comes into our lives for a certain amount of time. When they are no longer of use to us, they will be removed from our lives. With the heartbreak around not only certain romantic relationships, but all relationships, healing occurred and I was able to integrate more authentic feelings in my life. I was reminded that I have a lot of love in my heart to share with not only the right romantic partner but with all relationships.

Recently, I decided to revisit an exercise from my past. I made a list of the qualities I'm seeking in a romantic partner. These qualities had nothing to do with appearance, how much money they make, or what kind of car they drive. The qualities that resonate with me are more about a man's heart and head. Things like honesty, integrity, willingness and the ability to be a grown-up were on the list, along with quite a few other items.

After completing the list, I realized I'm striving for those same qualities in myself. With this revelation, I know it's worth the much longer wait for someone who is able to be all in, chooses to make that emotional investment, and understands the meaning of partnership. This someone is just as much of a work in progress as I am, and when the time is right for us to meet, it will happen. Until then, I continue to evolve, grow, and strengthen, gaining wisdom from each relationship along the way.

CHAPTER FOURTEEN

Question For Men (Or Women, For That Matter): Why Lie?

Here's an oldie but goodie from the joke archives: How do you know a man is lying? His lips are moving and sound is coming out of his mouth. (Pause for laugh) I'm sure men tell the same joke about women too, by the way.

I'm not a man hater and I'm not bitter about men. But it does get frustrating sometimes to encounter men who choose not to be truthful. Let's not even sugarcoat it. Men lie. It's that simple. And there's no rhyme or reason for why they lie. But they create an atmosphere of distrust the minute they do it with anyone, especially women. More's the pity though, because too many women (myself included at times, sad to say) are willing to believe the lie! I have worked hard to live in my truth. So it's disheartening when I encounter men who are less than truthful.

Men have different ways of lying. Some are outright liars and they are manipulative enough to make it seem like we're the ones with the problem if we catch them in a lie. I once was dating someone who it turns out was continuing a relationship with an ex-girlfriend even though I said it was a deal breaker for me. I found out about it, confronted him and he did nothing. But that's when I needed to end the relationship. Did I do that? No, I continued to date this man for what seemed like an eternity. Actually, we were together only two and one-half years, but when they are not happy ones, they can seem like forever, right?

Some men choose to lie by omission. Here's an example. I know a man who has a number of women interested in him romantically. He seems to be a nice, friendly, unattached guy. Or so we all thought. Recently he shared that he had been involved with a woman for a number of months. There were times when he was out with me or friends of ours on a weekend evening and when asked how did this fly with his girlfriend, his reply was "What someone doesn't know they don't have to be told, right?"

Further, he went on to say that he didn't consider this woman to be his girlfriend, even though they were physically involved. It was stunning to hear those words because it seems this man, who presented as a nice, unattached guy, is more of a player than anyone would ever have imagined. It's a little scary to know this man was out there, keeping his options open, so to speak, while being romantically (i.e. physically) involved with a woman.

Here's another one – the man who drops off the face of the Earth after a couple of good dates. Or the man who starts a relationship, and then runs with some story about being busy at work or not feeling attracted, or he doesn't miss you enough when he's not with you. While some of those reasons might be valid and might ring true, in my experience, the reasons came on the heels of a feeling or sense that the relationship was getting more serious (at least in my thinking) and the man involved was getting cold feet.

In the example of, "I just don't miss you enough when I'm not with you," this came from a man who made weekend plans to introduce me to his twin brother. Why would he make the plans to connect me to a family member if he doesn't miss me enough when we're apart? To me, the excuses all seem like "man speak" for the unwillingness to take a dating romance to the next level and make the commitment towards a long-term, monogamous, all-investment type of relationship.

It seems people will do almost anything to avoid being truthful in order to keep their options open. For me, monogamy is a requirement in any romance where there is a physical component and I make that clear right from the start. All fine and good, I'm choosing to speak my truth. But the responses I get are really interesting. And believe me, that use of the word "interesting" is not in a good way. A man I dated briefly said to me when that topic came up, "I've assessed the situation and I am comfortable with my decision." Needless to say there's a reason why I said we dated briefly.

Back to the question of why men lie. And by the way, I'm not saying women don't lie. They lie just as much as men. I don't even want to write down some of the excuses women I know have made when they don't want to say yes to an invitation. I used to be friendly with a woman who I thought was as invested in our friendship as I was. I started to get the clue that I was mistaken when I asked her to get together via text message. About three days later I got a return text that said she had just received my first text. I may have been born at night, but I wasn't born last night, and I'm adept enough with technology to know that was a lie. Bottom line? She didn't want to get together and she also didn't want to say no. So she lied. I was shown through her actions that my investment was wasted, so I cut her loose and moved on to find other friendships that were and still are much more reciprocal.

I think the basic thing is very few people are willing to say "no," or "no thanks." I have heard people tell me it sounds mean to say no. But what is worse – telling the truth with a polite "no" or "no thank you" or lying and then being found out? I'm OK with someone saying "no." Yes, it hurts my feelings a bit because if I ask someone to get together, it's because I truly want to spend time with that person. But if he or she says "no," I need to accept his or her choice and move on to make different plans for myself or with others. I don't always accept every invitation I get either, but I don't choose to lie about why I say "no." When a person lies about why he or she can't get together, it hurts. And it doesn't matter whether it's a man or a woman. A lie is a lie is a lie.

I send out the wish or belief that there are others along my life journey who strive for the same standards of honesty, integrity and authenticity that I try to maintain in myself. If it starts with me, then that has to be enough. If I continue the journey with those standards, then I will be rewarded by encountering others who believe the same. Here's hoping.

Chapter Fifteen
Reframing Rejection

Here's a favorite quote: "Man's rejection is God's protection." I'm comforted by this quote as I continue along in the dating journey. I've been rejected by people for whom I had begun to develop feelings, and I admit it hurts. It's never easy to be rejected, and it leaves me feeling sad, lonely and sometimes angry. At times I am relieved when something is over; other times I'm devastated. Obviously, it depends on the circumstances. But the rejection aspect of anything that ends is a hard pill to swallow.

In life there are always rejections – work situations, friendships, romances, even with family. Sometimes I'm the one doing the rejecting, other times I'm the one rejected. Intellectually, I can see the linear order when it comes to rejection. Something ends, feelings are hurt, loss is grieved and life moves on. Would that it were that simple, right? But actually, the heart, while resilient, also gathers this rejection and struggles to process it. And the feelings sometimes manifest themselves in other ways to make sure they are felt and dealt with.

An author whose work resonates with me has written a number of books that discuss the mind/body connection, which of course I'm all about. In the midst of my dating journey, a new body problem emerged in terms of pain in my right knee, and I did the rehab work to try to strengthen and heal it. But the pain continued to linger and sometimes I was able to see a direct connection between times when there was a flare up and my thoughts around men and romance in general.

I know this is a message from Higher Power about keeping the focus on myself and not get distracted or sidetracked by something or someone that won't bring long-term value to my life. In this way, I find it possible to reframe rejection. What a shame it is that I had to have a chronic physical ailment as a reminder to stay focused on my own direction and forward progress.

As I look back on my overall dating history I can see things like this sent to me before. Years ago at the end of one of my romantic relationships, albeit a very positive one, I was sent another physical ailment that required attention. And in that moment I was very clearly aware that my boyfriend at the time was not the right romantic partner for me in a permanent way. He was not able to be helpful to me in this very painful experience, which I was left to go through by myself.

At other times with other men, I've been sent physical obstacles and I can see these came to me as a reminder of my own life's importance. And each time these things happened, I was meant to go through them on my own. I am able to go through anything on my own, of course. But I'm realizing now that one of the things I'd like in a romantic partner is someone who would be there for me when I'm going through a difficult time. Is it a deal breaker? Let's call it a desire, a wish and a want.

As with many people, both men and women, I have a tendency at times to throw my own life over the side when I become involved romantically. Each time I found myself spending too much time focusing on the relationship vs. what I expect, need or want for myself, lo and behold, that man was removed from my life. Whether he walked away from me, or I already knew it would not last, I was left alone to heal, reflect, regroup and move on.

I'm no longer interested in throwing myself into a romantic relationship in such a way that it becomes a detriment to the rest of my life. I am all in when it come to love and romance, but the only way that works positively is if my own life is already in a place where it needs to be – regarding work, activities, physical and emotional health, friendships, etc. I have been on my own for quite some time and therefore forced to be focused on me. I did it happily because it helped me realize I am at a place where I know, appreciate and embrace how very special and wonderful my own life is already.

Instead of feeling upset or disappointed because of things that I don't have in my life, I have gratitude for everything I do have right at this moment and each day. And I am certain that my life needs to be exactly as it is for nobody else but me. Then and only then will I be sent the kind of romantic partner who will enhance, strengthen, and in all ways add to my life while not depleting anything from me or my own journey.

"Man's rejection is God's protection." There is gratitude for knowing I am responsible for my own happiness, and that all of my life is valuable right now, this minute, and I'm not alone. It's a feeling of peace and security knowing there is an order of things in life, and part of that "God's protection" sends me the message to trust the process, even when it starts as rejection. It's comforting to know if someone is removed from my life in the form of rejection, it's for my ultimate benefit in that the path is being cleared for something or someone else more wonderful to come along. For now, I'm still walking the solo path, but the route is clearly marked and the road is paved with positive intention. Onward!

CHAPTER SIXTEEN

WAIT (Walk Along In Trust) And HOPE (Heart Open Prayers/ Patience Extended)

As the dating process continues, I want to be able to WAIT (Walk Along In Trust), and HOPE (Heart Open Prayers Extended). I'm taking the time to reflect on both the WAIT and HOPE aspect of the journey toward lasting love.

For me HOPE also stands for Heart Open, Patience Extended. The dating journey is no different than any other life journey. It's a process, a trust thing, a one-day-at-a-time situation. When I started this latest chapter in my dating story, I was hopeful. At times I have been impatient and frustrated, wondering why I kept going out on first dates, and sometimes second and third dates, and sometimes even more dates than that, and nothing clicked. A little romantic glimmer here and there perhaps, sometimes feelings became invested, but so far nothing has led to a lasting, loving romantic partnership.

Whenever I think something romantic might be starting and then it doesn't work out, I feel sad, hurt and lonely. Sometimes I feel angry too, but that doesn't last very long.

Mostly it's the other three feelings of heartache that are closer to the surface. It's hard to go through this process of feeling the feelings again and again. It's uncomfortable and painful.

That's where hope comes in. With the knowledge that I keep hope alive, I'm able to get to gratitude for having met the person at all, to know he was sent to my life for a reason. Sometimes I don't know the reason, but eventually it becomes clear to me that I was given a gift.

This is not only true of romantic encounters, but also of friendships. Many times I found I needed to let go of friendships when it became clear that none of my needs were being met. It was all a one-way situation, with me doing the giving and the other person doing the taking. I hate when that happens, but at least I've learned through constant reminder and repetition of this situation that it's better to walk away sooner than to hang on to something where there is no reciprocal effort. Here's a good slogan: "What's the definition of insanity? Repeating the same behaviors over and over and expecting different results."

Recently someone told me to give up on hope in order to let go of desire and that way, the heart won't be hurt. But why would I want to protect myself from hurt? For me, hurt serves a purpose. The hurt lets me know that at least I have a heart that can feel and my feelings deserve to be felt, honored and validated. I don't want to close myself off from hope just to avoid being hurt. Rather, I choose to stay hopeful around many things in my life, not just romance. What is hope after all, but a willingness to believe in things going right, or working out, or coming to pass, or anything else positive?

I was told that concept comes from Buddhism's teachings. I don't know much about Buddhism, but that doesn't work for me. No matter how many times I may be shot down, no matter how many times I open my heart and life with the belief that someone right for me will walk into it, only to have that belief negated, I will continue to have Heart Open Patience Extended (HOPE). And if hope is the belief that things will work out somehow when that's meant to happen, along with HOPE must come WAIT (Walk Along In Trust).

That's a tough one, because I get impatient sometimes, and when I get impatient I know I stop trusting for a while. Again, along with the resilient belief in hope, I soon regain my trust and my willingness to let go of the outcome, which is what I need to do in order to keep with the whole concept of WAIT. In the lonely times when nothing is happening on the romantic front, or I've let go of a friendship that wasn't working, I feel the sad and scared feelings that go along with the impatience. I wonder why I'm by myself again, or why it seems as if I'm more on my own than closely connected to people. Then those thoughts give way to gratitude and I go back to being able to Walk Along In Trust (WAIT).

Ultimately, it's the trust factor that I'm being taught to embrace over and over. With each experience of letting go, I'm being shown how important it is for me to define my self-worth and to be true to my own needs. Frequently, I've let go of my own needs for the sake of someone else. I did this for years with family of origin relationships, based on the belief that if I kept modeling the caring and giving behavior it would come back around to me. Didn't happen. Then with certain friendships I thought if I did nice things, they would reciprocate. Didn't happen. And with certain past romantic partners, I believed if I demonstrated loving gestures, they would be returned to me. Didn't happen.

Through the decades of my life, the repeated reminder is I need to make my own life the primary focus and the ultimate number one priority. When I feel the shift of moving my life to a back burner, or the role of supporting player, that's when I know it's time to let go of whatever relationship is not meeting my needs, be it romance, friendship, family of origin member, client, colleague, whatever. I'm being shown what is required to be able to go slow, let go, relax and trust in the outcome one day at a time. It comes down to the same two concepts – Walk Along In Trust (WAIT) and continue to keep my Heart Open Patience/Prayers Extended (HOPE).

CHAPTER SEVENTEEN

Dating Without Desperation

I finally figured out how to date without desperation, and I have to say it gives me a whole new perspective to this dance of dating and relating with men. When I first decided to actively engage in the dating journey a while back, I thought I should take the in-with-both-feet approach. I put myself out there, threw myself into it, and right at the beginning had a three-week email correspondence with someone that I thought was going to lead to much more. I thought I'd gotten really lucky and had found someone so quickly that it must be fate or meant to be or whatever term you want to use.

After three weeks of intense lengthy emails, sometimes twice a day, this man started dropping hints about getting together in person. I said that would be nice and even went so far as to suggest we choose a time and place for a face-to-face meeting. Almost as soon as I did that, I got an email that said he realized we wanted different things and he was not in a position to be in the kind of relationship he knew I wanted, and all the rest of it.

Clearly, this man was doing a great job of game-playing, and unfortunately I fell for it. I know this man is available for dating (i.e., not married) because I know people who work with him. Regardless, he may have been available in terms of dating status, but just the same he wasn't emotionally available. And I'm sure I was one of many email pen pals with whom this man was corresponding.

Nevertheless, I refused to be discouraged, and continued my dating journey. There was a year-long period where I had a date with someone just about every weekend. Sometimes it was multiple dates with the same person; sometimes it was just one and done. And in between, there were email contacts, some phone contacts that seemed to be going toward something serious, and other phone conversations that spared me having to go meet someone in person.

Still, I continued, having dates every weekend, and it was emotionally exhausting. I would no sooner be able to protect my heart and move forward than a situation would present itself and I would be emotionally invested all over again, only to have the whole thing vanish like mist on a breeze. I kept thinking, "Maybe it's this one, maybe it's this one." But those maybes never turned into the real deal.

After a year of this exhaustive searching, I did a lot of thinking about how much this was intensifying my lonely, sad and angry feelings. But I kept thinking about how many people I knew who had done the dating deal and found the love they were looking for. What was their secret and why wasn't I getting clued into it?

I knew it was time to step back and take a different approach. I was not only aware of men on dating sites but also of men in activity groups I enjoyed. I was sending out messages of being open but also hearing the messages of self-care, self-worth and self-love. And with that, I became aware of how desperate I had been during the first year of dating. I was so intent on finding someone that I wasn't aware of how I wasn't connecting to myself and wasn't clear about my needs or emotional boundaries.

It took some doing, but I decided to stop initiating as much towards men. Instead, I took the approach of waiting to see who might initiate towards me. In the second year of the dating exploration I had far fewer dates. Sometimes it was the men who initiated and I had some lovely evenings. A couple of times I did decide to initiate and those were OK too. Once or twice a game-playing man showed up and I went along for the ride, but it didn't last as long and the fall wasn't as hard.

Remembering lessons learned long ago from other aspects of my life helped with my choice to trust the process. I firmly believe there is a larger presence in charge of all of this, and my only responsibility is to be in the place of strength to allow my heart to stay open. He's out there, and he and I will find our way to each other when that's meant to happen. But the meant-to-happen piece or timetable is not controlled by me or him. Now that it's out of my hands, the desperation is gone and I can date, relate and don't mind the wait.

PART FOUR

Here He Is: The Perfect One For Me

CHAPTER EIGHTEEN

Eight Words For Love

I think the word "love" is something we say too easily. What is the meaning of that word? We use it for everything, don't we? I love to travel, or I love that movie, or I love my home. That's all true, but is that what love is really about? When we're talking about romantic relationships, how is the word love intended?

I remember my first serious romantic relationship and how I knew my boyfriend wanted to tell me he loved me, but I think he was afraid to say it first in case I didn't say it back. I knew I loved him too but never had said that to anyone other than family before, so it was scary to say it for the first time. It was a very sweet and tender moment and one I have always treasured. The relationship didn't last a lifetime, but that memory does.

Sometimes the word love is said with fury, which seems completely paradoxical. I remember in another of my past significant romantic relationships, the first time we ever said, "I love you" to each other was in the midst of an argument! Not the best predictor of a bright and happy future, to be sure. To this day I am grateful that romance didn't last either, because it was full of red flags flying from the very first day. The two-plus years we spent together were very hard for me and though I learned much about myself, it certainly took its toll. And yet we said we loved each other. Definitely some irony in that situation.

In thinking about what the word love really represents, there are other words I hear in my head. They include (but are not limited to) patience, understanding, support, acceptance, regard/respect, admiration, value and cherish. These are the words I savor when thinking of love, how to love and who I love. I want those words to be present in any of my relationships – with colleagues, friends or romantic partners.

The words I associate with love aren't complicated, yet I see many relationships where it appears they are missing. I think about the relationships I have had with former friends, all of whom might have done the lip service of saying, "I love you" with one breath while harshly criticizing and verbally judging something about me with the next.

In my own experience, immediate family members have lied to me, verbally abused me, harshly disapproved of me, relentlessly criticized me, and were hurtful in general. Not quite what I would describe as love, and yet in our society we are supposed to use the word love when talking about family members. Seems hypocritical, doesn't it?

Fortunately, I have had some positive love relationships in my life from which I draw inspiration and strength. My father, now deceased, was the embodiment of the words I use to describe love. From the day I was born until the day he died, I was always certain of his unconditional love.

I'm grateful I had this type of relationship with at least one member of my immediate family, because as a result I have something to work toward in the rest of my relationships, including the most important one of all – the relationship I have with myself. And I continue to hold onto the belief that it is better to be on my own than to be settling for anything less than the qualities I associate with love. In any personal relationship, I choose today to wait for the ones where those words can be said, meant and felt.

Chapter Nineteen

The Websites Really Work!

This chapter's title speaks for itself, because I am happy to report that after using the dating websites for quite some time, I have found a true love and we are engaged to be married.

As I continued on the dating journey that led to this long-desired outcome, I resolved for probably the first time ever not to settle for anything less than what I knew would be right for me. That man didn't have a specific physical type, nor did he work a certain kind of job, or have a certain level of education. The qualities I knew to hold out for had to do with intangibles, but I believed more and more firmly that I would know those qualities when they were brought to me in the right man. That's exactly how it has worked out.

How do I know he is my true love? I can't explain that as accurately as some might like. So many people out there want the one formula or magic solution to lead them to their true love. Or they are asking, with increased desperation, "Will I ever find the true love I hope for, wish for, yearn for?" I know this because I was one of those people. I asked those questions over and over. I read the dating manuals and all of the self-help books about attracting love, finding love, keeping love, letting go of the wrong ones in order to be open to the right ones. You name it, I did it.

Why did it take me so long to stop settling, you ask? In my dating history I often was attracted to men who seemed comfortable or safe to me, but really what they turned out to be were familiar and known. What I mean by that is I became romantically involved with men whose characteristics echoed those of certain origin family members who routinely bullied and verbally abused me. After several of those types of men had come and gone, I went back to resolve some issues within those origin family connections. I had to do that self-exploration work in order to be very clear about what I would no longer tolerate or accept in romantic relationships.

All of this took years, but I finally figured out what would be right for me. With this most recent dating search, I was on a very different journey than in prior attempts. I finally got to a place where I was at long last comfortable with myself, accepting of whatever might happen (or not happen) in terms of permanent romantic partnership. I was absolutely certain that if I was meant to spend my entire life on this Earth without a permanent romantic partner, then that was going to have to be enough.

Did I hope that true love would come? Absolutely. I never stopped hoping, wishing, dreaming, or believing. At the same time, I knew and accepted that life without a permanent romantic partner would still be well-lived.

Doing this kind of focused dating brings the benefit of figuring out what doesn't work, and therefore being aware of what does work if/when it comes along. For example, I realized someone right for me would be like me in terms of lifestyle choices, like owning a residence, having gainful employment, and leading a grown-up existence.

As simple as they might seem, there are men out there who don't have even those essential building blocks. There are also the ones who are involved in way too much chaos on a daily basis. That might take the form of overindulgence in drugs and alcohol, entanglements with ex-wives and disruptive children, or enmeshed emotional care-taking relationships of any kind.

With all of this information in my head, I turned over the outcome and stayed open to the possible. With that, the quality of men I attracted or to whom I was attracted changed quite a bit. I didn't go on as many dates, but the ones I did agree to were with men who had better communication skills, had much more stable lives, and in general brought more to the table overall as potential life partners.

I also didn't limit my search to dating websites. I was open to whatever might happen, which meant I wasn't opposed to meeting the right man within an activity group, or at the grocery store, or wherever he might have appeared. The dating websites just allowed access to more options.

And after all of the trial and error, the right man entered my life and I knew almost instantly that he was the partner I had waited for all of these decades. So I'm here to say finding a true love is possible, does happen, and it's well worth the wait! My best advice? Don't stop believing!

CHAPTER TWENTY

I Got What
I Prayed For

What was it about this man that made me reach out to him in the first place? I never will be able to tell you why I chose to click send and let him know I was interested. From reading his profile, I thought we might not have very much in common, but that was never a deal breaker for me, as I've known many couples where the two were opposites. Was it his face, his eyes, his smile? I don't know, but for whatever reason, I thought it would be a worthwhile effort to let him know I was curious.

When he wrote back to me initially, I was impressed because he said he is never afraid to take a risk, and from the start he was self-disclosing which I found refreshing. As we corresponded over the next few emails, I kept looking for red flags in his delivery and/or message but could find none. I suggested we move to a phone call and he was thrilled and encouraged by that.

Our first conversation was shortly after our initial few emails on a Saturday evening. I liked that we were both home alone on a Saturday, and that neither of us felt like losers because of that. After chatting for two hours, we made plans to meet the following Friday afternoon. He checked in with me by email and phone the day before to confirm our plans.

On the afternoon of our first meeting, I arrived at the location first and waited for him. He walked up and we shook hands and started walking and talking together. From the first moment I felt a comfort and safety with him that is hard to describe. I also knew I was attracted to him; I liked the sound of his voice and how he carried himself.

As we strolled along, I found myself walking close to him and the pace of our walk and our conversation was easy and relaxed. At one point we got caught in a thunderstorm and after a flash of lightning, there was a crack of thunder that startled me; I reached out instinctively and grabbed his arm. I had known this man only for an hour, yet I knew without a doubt that he would protect me from danger.

We decided to go for dinner, where our nonstop conversation continued. Then he walked me to my car where we continued talking for a while longer. We set up a date for the next evening, and then we had our first kiss. There was magic in that kiss, and I knew that kiss and this man were something special. I drove home with a quiet feeling, a certainty inside me that I had just experienced my last first kiss. It wasn't the elation or giddiness of infatuation. It was something at a much deeper level, a feeling I knew I'd never felt before but wanted to keep feeling forever.

The next night we had another wonderful date with lots more talking. We shared our stories and found out we have so many things in common. We ate dinner and held hands and had another nonstop conversation and there was more kissing. It was romantic, and relaxed and lovely. Though neither of us wanted the evening to end, we knew it was best to say good night and make plans to get together again.

Two days later he called and told me he wanted to be all in and see where this relationship might go and was I game for that too? I said, "Yes."

By the end of that first week we had said, "I love you" to each other (he said it first). By the end of a month I knew I wanted to make a permanent future with him. By the end of two months he asked to have a conversation where he said the same thing. By the end of three months he asked me to marry him and again I said, "Yes."

Does this seem fast, like a whirlwind? You bet. Should I have had doubts or been more cautious? I don't know, because at no point since meeting this man has any of this felt hasty, rushed or in any way unsafe. We are in love; we both feel it equally, and we want to spend the rest of our lives together with gratitude and appreciation for being brought to each other. All I know is if I could have ordered this man from a catalogue, I couldn't have made a better choice.

So what was it? What was the magic formula that made this one click, that made this situation what I'd always hoped for? I can't say for sure, but I know all of the trial and error throughout my 40 years of dating served a purpose.

By virtue of decades of experience in identifying what doesn't work (what I don't want), I was very clear about what would work for me in a permanent relationship. I have been proposed to before, but something always stopped things short of really moving forward. There was always a red flag, a reason to hesitate, or to walk away. This time there was none of that. I listened to my heart and my head and they were aligned, probably for the first time.

I believe in a Higher Power that guides my life, and sends me everything I'm meant to have, whether positive or negative. Sometimes that comes in the form of major challenges, like job loss, or changes in friendships, or the endless stream of dates and romances with men who were wrong for me.

My Higher Power has guided my footsteps toward greater joy as well, like with my move from Pennsylvania to Colorado, where I found my true home. I often say moving to Colorado from Pennsylvania was moving from a life lived in black and white to a Technicolor one, and with that came contentment, fulfillment and joy.

And all of this awareness happened before this best romantic partner came into my life. All it took was choosing to trust the guidance and follow that to the best of my ability. When I realized I had done that with every other aspect of my life, I was able to do it with the romantic journey, and I was sent the gift of this man. As the title of this chapter states, I got what I prayed for. It was worth the wait.

CHAPTER TWENTY-ONE

Letting Go Of Life Alone

I had my own room growing up as a child. I had roommates who had off-campus boyfriends the first couple of college semesters, and then I had a single room for the rest of my college experience. I had one roommate after college. We shared a three-bedroom townhome and we each had a bathroom of our own. At 26 years old I started living in my own residence. I acknowledge I like my privacy and my time to myself. I admit I really enjoy just being alone.

In all of my romantic relationships, I may have spent time at someone's home or had him come to my home, but never did I choose to live with a man with whom I was romantically involved. Now, for the first time, I'm choosing to live with a man and share space with him in this new chapter of my life called marriage.

It's a little scary to be sure, but I admit it's something I've always thought about, wondered about, perhaps even wished for. I've wondered what it would be like to sleep in the same bed with a man every night and wake up with him every day. I've wondered what it would be like to come home from work to someone being there instead of an empty house. I've wondered what it would be like to share a refrigerator, closet, bathroom, living space, and ultimately a life built by two people together.

It's such a contrast to living my life on my own, and always a foreign concept until now. I'm used to making my own plans, arranging my own schedule, having the run of my alone space, being able to do what I want, when I want and how I want. This whole being with someone else on a permanent basis – especially in a shared residence – is definitely daunting.

Sometimes I wonder what it's going to be like to be around my future husband all the time. It's not as if we work together or are going to be together 24/7, but still it's quite something to think that after a lifetime of being a single (meaning unmarried) person, I'm going to be a wife with all that title implies.

Of course I'm over the moon about this dream come true in my life. I never knew how much I wanted this until it happened for me. I met a man who I knew from the first moment I could build a life with, and that he would be for me as I always hoped and imagined – a strong, confident, secure, vibrant, honest, thoughtful, willing partner.

As we are in the process of combining our households, we find we work very well together. We see a task and figure out how best and most efficiently to get it done. I am going to live with a grown-up and that's really what I was waiting for.

There are many people in the world who don't know how to function as grown-ups emotionally or intellectually, or in terms of being able to partner another person. I was pretty sure I was capable of being a grown-up partner to a man, but I kept running into men who were not capable of that kind of partnership. Some men were closer than others to the ultimate mark, but they all fell short until the man who was able to be that partner was sent to my life. And now he's arrived and it's pretty amazing and sometimes unbelievable. I am grateful for the gift of this man in my life, and for every day we get to be together.

I was prepared to do the alone thing forever if that was what was meant for me. But the hopeful romantic inside me always wanted to believe a partner would be sent someday to experience the love I have to share. Since that is happening, I can see now that with the right partner, the joining of lives doesn't need to be scary, difficult or fraught with obstacles or complications. With the right partner, it's a choreographed dance where the steps are known by both, and it's in perfect time to the music that only they can hear. Let the music play on!

Chapter Twenty-Two

A Change In Emotional Real Estate

From the moment I decided to make the move to a new part of the country, I recognized I not only was making a change in my physical location, but also it was for the good of my emotional health.

As a child I didn't have the choice of where I got to live, any more than I had the choice of the family into which I was born. I believe my Higher Power placed me into my origin family for many reasons, the most important of which is so I would have a life on Earth. I also was meant to learn things about myself from being a part of this particular family – like how to find the means to step out of it and become my own person. I learned to take what I liked from what I was taught in that family and to leave the rest. Still working on that one sometimes.

Memories of my childhood are mixed, but the overall feeling for me was one of unhappiness. I felt oppressed in my parents' house growing up for a thousand different reasons. Most importantly, I always felt under my mother's control. It started when I was 7 and she beat me with a kitchen mop. From that moment she owned me emotionally and mentally. She took my power from me and it took me years to get it back.

Even though my mother never physically abused me again, there was emotional and verbal abuse that continued for decades. For what seemed like forever, I did everything I could to please her and became a people pleaser for everyone else as well. My thought was at least I could please others if I couldn't please her. The seeds of codependent rescuing caretaker were sown in that moment of the physical abuse, and beyond that, the verbal, mental and emotional abuse went on for a very long time.

As an adult, my awareness is I allowed this codependent manipulation to continue. It was perpetuated by my believing what I was brainwashed to believe – that without my mother in my life, I would be somehow incapable of taking care of or supporting myself. And I hadn't yet figured out that I needed a network of support made up of truth-telling friends and perhaps a worth-waiting-for romantic life partner to tell me otherwise.

So I perpetuated the isolation created by my mother – no man is ever good enough, no friendships can ever be counted on, nobody is trustworthy except her, etc. etc. Today I can see how sick and twisted this thinking is and how ready I was to believe it, like a baby bird that opens its beak for the mother to give it food. My beak was wide open, but what I was being fed wasn't emotionally nutritious, healthy or even true!

My dad was a mainstay in my emotional well-being. When he died a number of years ago, I wondered why my

Higher Power would take from me the one parent on whom I could depend. The answer came back that his journey on Earth was completed, and I was meant to continue working on creating a relationship between me and my mother that would make better sense. That wasn't going to happen while my dad was alive, because he served as the middleman between us.

Further, I know he was removed because I did the necessary work in acknowledging I allowed myself to be a buffer for him as well. If my mother was emotionally and verbally manipulating me, then my dad was out of the line of fire. At one point, he and I discussed this situation, and I told him I would not continue as his emotional protection from her. He understood and we moved on from there. He was the parent who had no interest in agendas or emotional hostage taking. I called him out and we worked through it.

My mother is a narcissist, or at the very least has narcissistic tendencies. The textbooks say many things about that kind of person, but the bottom line is their words cut like knives and their actions leave their victims breathless and exhausted. They have all kinds of hidden agendas and everything is done with manipulation and subterfuge. My mother doesn't have the capacity to be the kind of loving parent who accepts, respects and cherishes her children.

It's sad to know I have a living parent with these issues. After many years of attempting to improve the relationship between us, I finally accept there is no effort to reciprocate coming from her side, because she is incapable of being connected with me in a healthy emotional way.

For a long time I allowed this emotional real estate to take up a lot of room inside my head. It was a large space, fully furnished with feelings of obligation, remorse, regret, resentment, anger, hurt, confusion, and overwhelming sadness. I lived within 20 miles of my parents for decades and even after I moved to the West, I was still living in the emotional real estate set up by my mother. I couldn't let go of it because I was getting something out of it. I think it was about my continuing to believe my mother could somehow change into the kind of parent figure I knew I wanted in my life.

Sometimes I believed my mother was changing for the better. She underwent surgery once and I watched over her as she struggled to come out of recovery, having been overmedicated by her surgical team. She was lying in her hospital bed and I remember she said to me, "You're such a good person, Valerie." At the time I remember the little girl inside me thinking she was capable of being loving and kind toward me with that statement. Yet the adult person in me was thinking, "Why does it take her being completely drugged for her to be so unguarded and say something positive to me?"

There are other positive memories I recall. She came along once to hear me speak at a national professional conference. It was thrilling to have her in the audience to witness the applause of 500 colleagues and to observe me in one of my professional roles. On that occasion though, she insisted on throwing a hissy fit when we went to a restaurant for dinner that evening and she didn't like anything on the menu. Once again, it had to be all about her.

To compound the issues of our complicated enmeshed relationship yet further, I chose to own houses with my mother for a number of years. The arrangement was for us to buy a house together, and thus I would have a place to live. Of course with 20/20 hindsight, I recognize this was a way for her to control me and also keep me believing that without her financial sponsorship, I would not be able to make it on my own.

I also believe this was a way for her to prevent me from really committing to a romantic partnership that could lead to marriage. In fact, when my fiancé and I got engaged, he and I decided after talking about our options that it would make the most sense for me to move into the house he already owned, and we would rent out or sell the one where I had lived.

Since my mother was a half-owner of my house, I needed to consult with her as to what would be done with the property. In these discussions, my mother said. "I think your fiancé is marrying you for my money." Wow, that was deep. Somehow this man who has worked hard all of his life and earned his own way in the world was suddenly after me for HER money? Really?

The decision became abundantly clear that the only course of action would be to sell this property, split the proceeds, and be able to step way back from someone who I already knew was toxic. The little girl inside me didn't want to walk away from my "mommy" – that little girl wanted to continue to believe that somehow, in some way, this woman could turn into the kind of "mommy" I wanted – loving, kind, caring, supportive, accepting of my choices, etc. But it was not to be, and ultimately it was the right decision to divest of the financial connection between us that led to so much of the emotional hostage taking in many of my adult years.

Fortunately, gratefully, with a lot of hard work, I came to understand I could be blessed with other parent figures in my life who are more than capable of connecting with me in the way I need. They demonstrate love, understanding, acceptance, support, celebration, admiration, respect and regard. I am aware that this is one of the gifts my father gave me, in that he did the same thing in seeking out other mentors in his life if/when his parents were incapable of giving him the emotional support he needed.

With this awareness, I am able today to let go of that old emotional real estate in which I was residing, despite my putting actual physical distance between myself and my mother. I was able to find my way into a new and beautifully decorated place of love, respect, acceptance, support, kindness, and happiness reflected back to me by my wonderful fiancé and the other friendships and acquaintances who occupy this new and beautiful space with me.

Was my fiancé being brought to my life a catalyst for being able to make this change? Yes, of course, but without the work I was already doing, the willingness to be open to this special and amazing man would not have been there. Everything that was meant to happen had a timetable, and that was set up and managed by the Higher Power who loves and protects me even in the midst of putting me in what seemed like harm's way with my relationship with my mother. It may have been harm, but from that harm I found my way to healing. I was able to come to settlement, let go of my old emotional real estate, and take up residence in a new life that is full and rich and wonderful and happy. A valuable and worthwhile transaction.

Chapter Twenty-Three

My Turn For A Wedding

It's finally happening for me, and it's an out-of-body experience in a way. I just attended my bridal shower, and it was totally amazing and so surprising and I still can't believe it's real.

I have been going to weddings since I was a child. Then in my 20s, as everyone I knew seemed to be running to couple with someone, I went to way too many bridal showers and weddings and all things connected. Then I went to more weddings in my 30s and 40s, and I remember sitting at many of them with tears in my eyes, feeling sad for the thought of always being at someone else's wedding and never at mine.

The last wedding I attended was in my 50s, and I remember thinking while watching the couple say their vows how it seemed like a staged play. I also remember thinking I could never imagine doing that kind of thing in front of other people. I don't know that I'd reached a place of acceptance or belief that I would never get married, but I was in a different head space about it than I'd ever been before.

And now it's my turn for a wedding, and the other wedding events like my bridal shower, where I wore the dress-up veil and crown and sash. I sat in a circle and opened gifts. People took photos of me. We went to lunch and toasted my special day. It was all for me, all about me, and is this really real? All this time when I've been engaged, I look at my engagement ring and I think "Whose hand is this wearing that ring?" Seems unbelievable sometimes that it's really happening in my life – the life always lived as a single, never-married woman. Wow.

It's been quite the whirlwind for me, doing all of the typical and sometimes traditional things connected with a wedding. My fiancé and I went shopping for rings together. I was calm sitting in the jewelry store, choosing a ring to wear every day for a lifetime, not really able to take in how significant that is. Wearing the ring has been emotional sometimes. At first I was conscious of how odd it felt to have a ring on that finger, which I'd always intentionally left bare. But after a while I adjusted to it, and now if it's not on my hand, it feels odd not to be wearing it.

My fiancé and I talked about planning our wedding. He was in on everything from the start – how many people to invite, what was our budget, where we would be married, and what we both wanted. It's been a collaboration from the beginning. He knew I was the kind of woman who had always imagined a certain wedding scenario. At one point he asked me had my vision changed much since my younger days and actually the answer was no. The venue is different and so is the time of day, but other than that, most everything is as I visualized it years ago.

We designed the invitation and prepared the invitation packets together. We visited with the wedding venue managers and all of the other vendors together. It's been a together experience and it's gone smoothly as we both participated equally. This is the reason why he's the one for me. It's that partnership I'd been dreaming of, yearning for, believing in my whole life. It's finally become real and true.

We're almost at the big day at this point and whenever I say that out loud, there's this little tingle that runs down the back of my neck. It's not a bad thing, more about the anticipation and the whole "who would have ever thought this would really happen?" kind of dialogue that goes on inside my head.

In my heart of hearts, my "hope for happily ever after" heart, I always wished this would happen. But the decades of being single and disappointed in so many prior attempts at lasting romance created some cynicism and disbelief that the right life partner would ever find his way to me.

When I moved to the West, I had no sense that I was moving to find the love of my life. I heard the call, so to speak, and knew it was the right decision and the right timing. I came to Colorado without knowing anyone, and established my life in every facet and aspect. I found work, made friendships, became involved in my favorite activities, and eventually went back out there with dating again.

Perhaps putting things in that order of priority was part of the reason why ultimately, my fiancé was brought to me. Perhaps it was my willingness to turn things over to the larger-than-I-am presence that I allow to guide my life. For me I describe this as my Higher Power. But it could also be thought of as God, or the Divine or the Universe – that's entirely up to the individual. In any event, the unfolding journey that is my life has led me to this set of events that I always dreamed of as a little girl.

Who knew I had so much of that little girl inside me? She's still in there and giggling with delight as the wedding events and wedding itself draws near. That little girl is as much a part of me as the evolving grown-up woman. I work toward integrating them together to create the authentic woman I choose to be in my daily life.

Chapter Twenty-Four

First-Time Bride At Last

I'm a first-time bride at 55, and I now have a husband! Who could have imagined that would happen to me? I may have had hope in my Cinderella heart, but I didn't know if it ever would come true. And now it has and I'm married. Sometimes I struggle with the belief that Higher Power has a plan far better than any I could ever imagine. Often I've heard the slogan "God's time, not mine." But being human and wanting things when I want them, I sometimes was reluctant to really believe. But as in many instances before and I'm sure many more yet to come, the plan that came true was in fact the best one of all.

How can I find enough superlative words to describe the magic and beauty that was my wedding day? There are so many thoughts and feelings inside my head – reminders of the memories created on that day. It's an event I prayed for, hoped for, thought about, wrote about, and wondered about. Everything leading up to the event and the event itself were all beyond my wildest dreams.

In the weeks just before the event, there were many details to finalize and the tasks all got completed. In the few days before the wedding, I felt the butterflies of anticipation. That was such a new feeling for me. I've had nervous anticipation before for other reasons, but never for this. In the days before our wedding we had other social events that helped build the anticipation. We spent time with family members and good friends at dinners and lunches and it was lovely to see their excitement for us and to share that positive energy.

The day of our wedding dawned with good weather, a huge gift for us since we'd planned an outdoor ceremony at a mountaintop location. My husband and I got ready and went to meet our photographer for some pre-wedding photos. I felt nervous just before we got in the car to drive to our ceremony location, but once we got there I felt calm, relaxed and happy. Some of our guests began to arrive, and they hugged us and took photos with us and it was warm, friendly and joyous.

Our ceremony started right on time and our friends and family assembled on the mountaintop. The sun shone down on us as we exchanged rings. After the ceremony there was an impromptu hugging reception line as our guests came to wish us well. One of my friends who is also single, in her 50s, and never married, said to me, "There's hope for all of us." My husband's sister told me she hasn't seen him this happy for many years. There was a shuttle bus for guests to be driven to and from the ceremony and then back to the reception. One of our friends told me that on the front of the shuttle bus was a marquee sign that said "Shinbaum/Lane Wedding." That's so cool!

Our reception site was an indoor space with outdoor access overlooking a lake with a mountain view beyond. Our guests gathered at inside and outside tables with food, and my husband and I gave a toast to welcome everyone. We had a piano player, and the rest of the evening was spent visiting with our guests and enjoying the wonderful energy of that experience. It was amazing to look around and see my favorite people all in the same place at the same time. That was the best wedding gift of all.

My husband told me that the whole week leading up to the wedding, and on the day and evening of the wedding itself, I was beaming with happiness. I have been looking at the photos and it's true. I have a smile on my face that I know was genuine and heartfelt. My new husband also said he could see the little girl inside who always dreamed of being a bride, and how happy he was that he caught frequent glimpses of her.

There was one note of disappointment and sadness. My mother chose not to attend the wedding. At first, she was going to come and sent her RSVP as a yes. Later on she changed her mind. I have no way to get inside her head and understand what motivated that choice, and it's not important or necessary for me to do that. I sit with the feelings of the little girl inside me who was constantly disappointed and hurt by her throughout my life.

With her decision not to be a part of this special experience, I am once again reminded of her inability to be the fantasy "mommy" I made up in my little girl head and heart. It would make better sense for me to believe in the reality of her limitations. Therefore, out of this sadness and disappointment came the recognition of the strength of Higher Power's love for me in the gift that was my mother's absence from our wedding. The day was all about me and my husband, our loving friends and gracious family members.

Now that this life-changing event has come and gone, what will the future hold? There was such a huge emotional buildup not only toward this experience with my husband around the wedding, but also in the prior "remaining single" lifetime before it filled with wondering, dreaming, thinking, planning, doubting and trying to continue believing it would happen.

I spent decades thinking I didn't need this milestone, that it wasn't for me, that I could live without it, that I was more than OK if it never happened, that I was doing fine on my own, that remaining single was a wise and well-thought-out choice. And that was all true.

As in all things, the plan for me was different, and I was being prepared through my own personal work to be ready for my husband to arrive, just as he was being prepared for me through his own work and life journey. We are together in life, sharing the same road going forward.

Remaining single until this moment was the ultimate right choice, even though it was more Universally driven than any way in which I could or needed to control the outcome. None of this would be possible without that willingness to accept what is, and believe in what could be.

Acknowledgments

This book came about with the assistance, guidance, love and support from a number of special people who grace my life. I believe they already know their value and worth in my journey, as it's through a lifetime of interpersonal connections that this book was brought into existence.

In addition to the helpful humans who shine like beacons, I give gratitude to my best source of inspiration, my Higher Power, with whom I choose to continue conscious contact one day at a time. I am honored and humbled to receive your gifts and blessings.

And with more love than I can ever describe, to my amazing, wonderful, loving husband – you are my life partner, my best friend, and my big strong man. You brought the best ending to this book and the greatest happiness to my life.

About The Author

Valerie J. Shinbaum, MS, is a Licensed Professional Counselor, a National Certified Counselor, and a Master Addictions Counselor, with two private practice locations in the Denver, CO metro area.

Ms. Shinbaum is a college professor, national conference speaker, author, and former radio talk show host.

To connect with Valerie,
visit **BodyMindAndBalance.com**

www.ingramcontent.com/pod-product-compliance
Lightning Source LLC
Chambersburg PA
CBHW020619300426
44113CB00007B/706